A CATHOLIC HOMESCHOOL TREASURY

A Catholic Homeschool Treasury

Nurturing Children's Love for Learning

Second Edition

Compiled and Edited by
Rachel Mackson and Maureen Wittmann

IGNATIUS PRESS   SAN FRANCISCO

First edition published in 1997
Spiritus Sanctus Books
Okemos, Michigan

Cover art by Christopher J. Pelicano
Cover design by Riz Boncan Marsella

© 1999 Rachel Mackson and Maureen Wittmann
Published by Ignatius Press, San Francisco, 1999
ISBN 0–89870–725–0
Library of Congress catalogue number 98–74071
Printed in the United States of America ∞

Dedications

To my father, Gregory New, my husband, Dave, and my children, Philip, Grace, and Emily. Each of you has my heartfelt gratitude, and my love, for the help and support you have shown.

—Rachel Mackson

To the Franciscan Sisters of Holy Ghost Grade School in Berkeley, Missouri, for teaching me about Christ and his Church, and to my beloved parents, Joe and Marirose Fagin, for continuing those lessons in our home.

—Maureen Wittmann

Contents

Acknowledgments

There are so many people to thank in the production of this book. First, we must give thanks to God for the gift of motherhood and for his guidance, and to the Blessed Mother for her example.

We are especially grateful to our families. They went beyond the call of duty in their understanding and helpfulness when dinner was not on the table or laundry was not put away because we were busy writing and editing.

The writers of the enclosed essays have our deepest appreciation. They opened their hearts and welcomed us into their homeschools. It is not an easy thing to share your trials and triumphs with the world.

Without the support of our fellow Catholic homeschoolers, we would have been lost when we began this journey. Therefore, we would like to thank all of our homeschooling friends for their advice, guidance, and support.

There are many friends and family members whose names do not appear elsewhere in this book, but whose imprint is everywhere. We offer thanks to all of our proofreaders—Ann Banke, R. Joseph Fagin, Marshall Fritz, Richard Nadler, Dawn Newton, The Skibas, Lloyd Sloan, The Wageners, and Denise Wahrer. Warm thanks go to Gregory New for sharing his editing expertise.

Finally, we offer a special thank you to Ron and Cindy Garrison for their generous contribution of printing services and supplies.

—RACHEL MACKSON
— MAUREEN WITTMANN

Introduction

We have produced this book to show what real-life homeschoolers do. There are certainly many ways to homeschool; from the structured curriculum to un-schooling, with all the permutations in between. Our purpose in compiling these essays is to give a sampling of how those in the trenches are successfully finding their way through the homeschooling maze. In these pages you will find the thoughts and ideas of many people. We, the editors, do not share every view expressed, but we feel called to give a voice to the rich variety of Catholic homeschoolers.

Please keep in mind that it is not our intent to tell anyone exactly how to homeschool. We offer this to you as a sampler of what homeschoolers are doing, wherever they are homeschooling. The methods vary, for each family eventually settles upon its own unique style. Nonetheless, a common theme runs throughout. We all desire to raise and educate our children within the family. And we wish to share with them the richness and beauty of our Catholic faith.

If you are new to homeschooling, there are probably many terms and styles of teaching with which you may be unfamiliar. We include below a brief section of helpful definitions to guide you when these terms are mentioned. To help you further, we have placed resource guides in the appendices, which include ordering information for many of the items mentioned in this book.

Helpful Definitions

Child-led learning: See *Unschooling*.

Classical education: Broadly, education according to ancient or medieval models. More important to the Catholic homeschooling tradition is the model from the medieval universities that defined the seven liberal arts. These were grouped into the trivium consisting of grammar, rhetoric, and dialectic (logic); and the quadrivium consisting of geometry, arithmetic, music, and astronomy.

Etymology: Study of the origin of words and their roots.

Eclectic homeschooling: An approach in which one chooses from various methods and philosophies that which appeals to and works best for the individual family.

Phonograms: Small phonetic sound units that make up English words. (*ow*, *ng*, *ou*, etc.)

Readiness: The level of maturity and the knowledge-base that children need in order to progress educationally.

Relaxed homeschooling: An approach between work-text schooling and unschooling (see below). The parents often delay formal academics and wait for a child to show signs of readiness. They combine child-led learning with parent-initiated work.

Scope and sequence: A formal grade-by-grade list of the skills and knowledge that children are expected to master in school. You can find a scope and sequence on the Seton Home Study School website (see Appendix C), in Kolbe Academy's general catalog, and in *The Core Knowledge Series* by E. D. Hirsch, Jr.

Spiral curriculum: Type of curriculum used by most schools. Topics are repeated through the years with greater depth each time. This repetition reinforces and builds upon the information and skills the students learned previously.

Unschooling: Term originally coined by John Holt, an educational reformer who has greatly influenced and helped the homeschooling movement. Whatever his original intent for the term, unschooling is now used to describe child-led learning. The underlying philosophy is that real life will provide a better education for children than textbook learning and that children are so drawn to make sense of the world they can be trusted to learn what they need to know, when they desire to know it.

Unit study: An approach that seeks to integrate learning by using a common theme throughout all subjects. Many people create their own modified unit studies by examining one topic in depth, while still using their main math and language arts texts.

Work-text schooling: Traditional textbook learning. Practitioners of this method seek to provide a thorough education to ensure that no educational gaps exist.

About the Editors and Writers

Editors

Rachel Mackson

Rachel and her husband, David, have three children, ranging in age from four to ten years. They are eagerly looking forward to their eighth year of homeschooling. The Macksons helped organize a local homeschool group, *Celebrating Home under Rome: Catholic Homeschooling* (CHURCH). CHURCH has grown to include more than ninety families. Rachel has also written for *The Catholic Home Educator*, a Catholic homeschooling magazine. The Macksons reside in Okemos, Michigan.

Maureen Wittmann

Maureen and her husband, Robert, are homeschooling parents of five children, Christian, age nine, Mary, seven, Laura, five, Joseph, three, and new baby, Gregory. Robert is a pioneer in the Educational Choice movement. Maureen is a free-lance writer who has been published in several homeschooling and Catholic periodicals. The Wittmanns are natives of St. Louis, Missouri, and now reside in Lansing, Michigan.

Writers

Beverly L. Adams-Gordon

Beverly and her husband, John, are homeschooling parents of three daughters. They reside in Lynnwood,

Washington. Beverly is editor and publisher of *Spelling Power* and other homeschooling books. (For more information, please see Appendix B.)

Lisa Gayle Brown
Lisa and her husband, Rick, have been homeschooling their three children, Amanda, Richard, and Michael, for two years and have registered with Kolbe Academy for the upcoming school year. They are active in their parish, and have taught religious education for two years. In addition, Rick is vice-president of their parish council. They are also considering starting a Catholic homeschool support group in their area. Lisa is the co-developer of the "Catholic Home Education Planner" and related products (see Appendix B). As a family, the Browns enjoy playing sports, particularly baseball and basketball, and they also take pleasure in playing music together. Lisa and Rick are lifelong residents of Frankfort, Kentucky.

William E. Brown
Mr. Brown and his wife, Natalie, are the homeschooling grandparents of Becky and Bill Wissner's four children. They reside in Midland, Michigan.

Lynne Cimorelli
Lynne and her husband, Mike, have unschooled their seven children, ages ten and under, since birth. They live on one beautiful acre, which overlooks thousands of acres of ranch land in El Dorado Hills, California, where they own and operate Cimorelli Construction and Alexander Publishing.

Patsy Conley
Patsy and her husband, Kevin, are homeschooling parents of six children, newborn to age nine. Patsy enjoys educat-

ing her children with the help of Kolbe Academy. They reside in Okemos, Michigan.

Kim Fry

Kim is the mother of five children and has been home-schooling for six years. She educates her children at home using a classical curriculum. She resides in Ogden, Utah, where her husband is with the Air Force.

Cindy Garrison

Cindy and her husband, Ron, are the parents of Ashley, twelve, and Drew, ten. Beginning their sixth year of homeschooling, they reside in Perry, Michigan. Family life centers on their parish, where they are involved in social ministries, lectoring, and serving where needed. They built their house on land that has been in the family for three generations and are busy planting a fruit orchard for future generations. Cindy is also the sales and market-ing director for *Heart, Mind, and Soul*, a Catholic home-school magazine (see Appendix B).

Laurie Navar Gill

Laurie and her husband, Douglas, are homeschooling parents of four children in suburban St. Louis, Missouri. Doug is a computer professional. The Gills publish *Home-front*, a monthly newsletter of practical tips and product reviews for Catholic homeschooling parents (see Appen-dix B.) Laurie is also the author of several books on Catho-lic traditions in the home, published by Gilhaus.

Sandra Heinzman

Sandra has been homeschooling her son, twelve, and daughter, eight, since 1993. She lived in Puerto Rico when she began homeschooling her son, who was in the second grade. She and her husband, Bob, are now homeschooling for religious reasons, and they feel it is the best option for their family. She has used Calvert School, Seton Home Study School, and an eclectic mix of her choosing. She considers herself a relaxed homeschooler. The Heinzmans plan to homeschool "as long as it works". They reside in Richmond, Virginia.

Dani Foster Herring

Dani and her husband, Michael, are homeschooling parents of three children. Dani especially enjoys using the Internet to supplement her homeschool program. They reside in Baltimore, Maryland. Dani has a web page designed for Catholic homeschoolers at www.geocities.com/~daniherring/.

Annie Kitching

Annie is a native of Boulder, Colorado. She and her husband, Craig, have been blessed with two children, Aidan, sixteen, and Lydia, twelve. Annie has served as director of religious education at St. Thomas Aquinas Parish in East Lansing, Michigan, for eleven years. Craig is a teacher and counselor at Lansing Catholic Central High School. The family is active in sports, the Irish-American Club of Lansing, and Advent House Ministries.

Sue Kreiner

Sue and her husband, Tom, have been blessed with ten children. They educate their children at home using a variety of resources. They reside in Portland, Michigan.

David C. Mackson

David and his wife, Rachel, are homeschooling parents of three children. David is a packaging engineer. They reside in Okemos, Michigan.

Julie McCaskill
Julie and her husband, Dan, have just completed their first
year homeschooling using Seton Home Study School with
their daughter, Juliana, age fourteen. Their challenge this
year has been homeschooling an only child (they have a
college-age son who lives out of town) in a geographic area
that has few homeschooled teenagers. They reside in Red-
wood City, California, which is 35 miles south of San
Francisco.

Marcia Neill
Marcia and her husband, Joe, are homeschooling parents
of four children. Marcia is also the director of St. Michael
the Archangel Academy in Orange County, California,
with 73 homeschool families and 168 students (see Appendix B).

Mark and Julie Stenske
Mark and Julie are homeschooling parents of four children. They reside in Lansing, Michigan, and are active in
their parish, in prolife activities, and in promoting the
Faith. Mark has been quoted in *Our Sunday Visitor*.

Karen Urness
Karen and her husband, Tim, are homeschooling parents
of five children, ages two to thirteen. They reside in Bur-
lington, Wisconsin, and recently finished their eighth year
of home education. Karen has written for *Sursum Corda!*—
a Catholic magazine that includes an excellent sixteen-
page homeschool spread—and for *Catholic Digest*. (For
more information about *Sursum Corda!* see Appendix B.)
The Urness family has its own web page at www.
geocities.com/Heartland/Acres/3595/catholic.htm/.

Richard and Colleen Wheat

Richard and Colleen are beginning their third year of formal homeschooling with their two children. Patrick will be starting first grade, and Maggie will be in a preschool program. They are trying a classical style this term, after their first year of combining a preschool curriculum and hands-on learning. The Wheat family resides in Lansing, Michigan.

Becky Wissner

Becky and her husband, Bill, have been homeschooling for seven years. The Wissner home is filled with the beautiful voices and artistic masterpieces of Becky and Bill's four children, age eighteen months to eleven years. They reside in Lansing, Michigan.

Soul of a Child

Rachel Mackson

Open your eyes and you will see
    The beautiful soul of a child.
Hungry for love, thirsty for knowledge,
    Unfolding one petal at a time.

Fragile, be careful, so easy to crush,
    But also so easy to lead.
"Show me!" it says, "Show me the world."
    "Show me the Way, and the Word."

The way of the cross, the way of the Truth,
    Echoes the echo of agony.
But the way of the cross, the way of the pain,
    Is also the way of love.

So open your eyes and you will see
    The beautiful soul of a child.
Fragile, ethereal, heavenly light,
    Waiting for the Truth to be told.

Chapter 1

Off to a Good Start

To be Queen Elizabeth within a definite area, deciding sales, banquets, labors, and holidays; to be Whitely within a certain area, providing toys, boots, cakes, and books; to be Aristotle within a certain area, teaching morals, manners, theology, and hygiene; I can understand how this might exhaust the mind, but I cannot imagine how it could narrow it. How can it be a large career to tell other people's children about the Rule of Three, and a small career to tell one's own children about the universe? How can it be broad to be the same thing to everyone and narrow to be everything to someone? No, a woman's function is laborious, but because it is gigantic, not because it is minute.

—G. K. Chesterton

At the Crossroads
Marcia Neill

Five years ago, our family began with prayer, as many families do, searching for educational alternatives for our four children. We were at a crossroads. The increasing tuition at our Catholic school had outpaced our income. We desired a Christ-centered education for our children and found public schools were not an option. We began a novena for guidance. Within a week, we met several homeschooling Catholic families. What caught my attention were the courteous, considerate manners of the children. They spoke easily with adults and children of all ages.

We began to consider home education. We took the summer to attend homeschooling conferences and found support for our family's decision in the encyclicals of Pope John Paul II: "Since they have conferred life on their children, parents have the original, primary, and inalienable right to educate them; hence they must be acknowledged as the first and foremost educators of their children" (*Charter of the Rights of the Family*, 1983, art. 5).

By September, we formed St. Michael the Archangel Academy to serve Catholic families using independent study programs. Twenty-one students from seven families were enrolled. In home-educating families, the mother is usually the primary instructor, the father is the administrative support as principal in the home, and the children are the students. With a Scope and Sequence chart showing what students typically learn in each grade as a guide, the parent instructors choose curriculum formats and instruction styles to match the learning styles and special needs of the children.

Our first goals were to foster the art of learning and develop thinking skills in our children while covering the four R's: religion, reading, 'riting, and 'rithmetic. Our four children, then in pre-kindergarten, fifth grade, eighth grade, and tenth grade, were ready to start school. We had new pencils, notebooks, and the textbooks that we had collected during the summer. We began each day by attending the 6:30 A.M. Mass. Beyond the spiritual benefits, going to Mass got the children up and dressed each day. We met other home-educating families whom our children looked forward to seeing and visiting. Within a few months, our friends were commenting on our children's self-assurance.

When we first started, my spiritual director told me that if the only accomplishment we had the first year of homeschooling was the religious formation of the children, we could consider our endeavor a success. Pondering what brought us to homeschooling and what motivates us to continue leads me back to the first time we knew we had made the right decision. It was a Saturday, and our whole family went on a field trip for the experience of learning how to pick apples and glean corn from the fields. We met at a park and began by praying midday prayers with other families. This alone was unique, praying publicly in a park. We had our picnic lunch and then went to pick apples at Riley's farm. The field trip was a singular day for us. The focus was on the family. We all felt fulfillment and enjoyment in an activity designed for the whole family.

It was a stark comparison to where we had been the previous year, when our children were enrolled in traditional schools. Our family of six struggled with being pulled in six different directions, each member having his own activities. There was just not enough time. Balance between activities was lost as the high-school student experienced the me-attitude of expecting transportation to distant events. Parents spent hours volunteering away from the home to be closer to and have some impact on the children's lives. The family home was lost as we became six individuals functioning from a base unit, the house.

Homeschooling is a family activity that is more than an educational system. Families soon learn that teamwork is necessary for success and that the team involves more than the individuals within the family. The education of children is an activity around which the family nourishes the soul as well as the body. We know that within our soul lies our intellect and free will, whose goals are to know, love, and serve God. The emphasis of homeschooling is the intellect, as well as moral formation to guide the child's will. Although religious formation is our main goal, we have been gratified by our recent achievement testing, which was successful, thus demonstrating the academic rewards of time spent forming our children.

Love nurtures the members of the family and motivates them to do their best for each other and for God. Humble prayers petition God for help, for virtues, and for graces to succeed where on our own we would fail. From the prayerful respect shown to the Supreme Authority flows the respect given to each person within the family and to other families.

When we consider what a gift our families are to us, we dare not take them for granted. We live in such a lonely society. Oh, there are thousands, even millions of people surrounding us. Our homes are lined up on the streets with other homes with neighbors we do not know. Even within our own homes, we can be so busy that we miss having the time to know each other. Having time together is the big advantage of homeschooling. The success depends on our humility and love. Homeschooling challenges the way we interact within our family and with other families.

And he said to him, "You shall love the Lord your God with all your heart, and with all your soul, and with all your mind. This is the great and first commandment. And a second is like it, You shall love your neighbor as yourself. On these two commandments depend all the law and the prophets."

—Matthew 22:37–40

Socialization
Maureen Wittmann

I am a homeschooling mother of five. Recently, a friend asked me the question that everyone asks, "What about socialization?" "Yes!" I shouted excitedly. "Yes, that is exactly why I homeschool." Judging by her perplexed stare, I do not think that was the answer she expected. She was surprised to find that homeschooled children are indeed actively engaged in the local community.

My homeschooled children are not being deprived of social experiences. In fact, I do not think that my children are any less socialized than their public- or private-school peers. Rather than learning how to socialize with twenty-five other first-graders, my son is learning how to interact with people of all ages. And we hope he is learning how to be an individual.

Because I do not have the profound responsibility of keeping so many little ones motivated and disciplined, formal schoolwork takes less time for me and for my children. This allows us to get out of the classroom and experience real life. I do not have to worry about permission slips and scheduling transportation. I can load my kids into our trusty minivan, and we are off on an impromptu trip to local points of interest. Since we can take school with us, we have been able to experience museums and cultural events in other cities as well.

My children have ample opportunities to interact with other children. Local homeschool support groups have so many organized activities families are able to pick and choose. There are academic clubs, organized sports, community service organizations, social clubs, and more. Of course, there are our neighborhood friends too. It is not uncommon to pass our house and see five to ten kids playing together.

We socialize with a diverse group of people. Homeschoolers come from a variety of cultural, religious, and economic backgrounds. I believe that by promoting educational choices we are adding to the cultural richness of our society. Kids in public schools, private schools, and homeschools all have something unique to offer our society.

As you can see, my homeschooled children are not leading a sheltered life. Yes, my husband and I hold them close, but they will fly when they are ready. In the meantime we are able to foster their emotional security. We are protective of the children. We know that the day will come when they are faced with pressures to try drugs or to engage in sexual activity before marriage. We will do our best to protect them until they are prepared to face those pressures head-on.

Someone once told me that the moral child is the socialized child. We cannot expect our children to play and share with others if we do not teach them basic rules of moral conduct, such as not to steal and not to lie. We strive to teach these lessons and set a good example in our home.

Is homeschooling for every family? No, but it's right for our family, and socialization is only one of the many reasons we love homeschooling.

Finding Our Niche
Rachel Mackson

I am in the unique situation of having been homeschooled as a child, for one year, while living overseas. Thus, when I decided to homeschool my own children, I automatically sent for materials from Calvert School, the program my mother had used. I did not know that Catholic curricula existed. Calvert supplies a detailed, thorough package filled with creative teaching tips, but even so, I desired a more Catholic alternative. I soon heard of Seton Home Study and was elated to find that the director, Mary Kay Clark, had written *Catholic Home Schooling*. Her advice on Catholicizing our home and curricula was inspiring.

Covering the basics was the focus of my early homeschooling. My son was not ready for a formal first grade or lots of written work since his motor skills and ability to sit quietly were still developing. For academic direction, I followed the advice of Seton and used the secular math workbooks by Modern Curriculum Press (MCP). These workbooks incorporate basic arithmetic and simple problem-solving, but I wanted more for our math studies. I bought a set of pattern blocks and played card games like blackjack with my children to reinforce addition and subtraction skills.

I was unsure, however, about teaching a child to read and was often caught short by my son's questions. Fortunately, a friend recommended *Sound Beginnings*, by Julia Fogassy. This program, which can be purchased from the Emmanuel Books catalog, offers specific, easy-to-use suggestions. To round out this first-grade curriculum, I ordered *Child's Bible History*, *The Usborne Complete First Book of Nature*, and *Our Life with Jesus* (*Faith and Life* series) and read them out loud.

We continued, studying in fits and spurts; taking breaks as needed for the birth of a baby or the myriad interruptions that life throws at a family. We pursued passing enthusiasms where they took us, and these surprisingly produced a great deal of learning. Mostly, I read books to the children. There were many days when I felt that nothing educational was accomplished, but we made steady progress. Occasionally, one of my children had a sudden burst of insight or showed signs of deep thinking, but for the most part we plugged away like the Little Engine That Could.

Around the time of my son's second-grade year, I felt confident in my ability to cover the basic subjects and ventured further afield. In searching for products to enliven our schooling, I managed to waste quite a bit of money. Then one day, as I was reading *The Tortoise and the Hare* aloud to my children, I was struck by the parallel to homeschooling. Children do learn in giant leaps and bounds, which is valuable. But my role as a homeschool teacher was to help the children persevere during the slow times. Our small amounts of daily study were adding up.

This insight was the turning point in our homeschooling. I could relax knowing that there was no need to rush through our studies. As long as the child excelled academically, we could take our time because intelligence does not go away. On the other hand, if the child was behind in a subject, we could still make slow and steady progress that would win in the end. This revelation led me to stick with basic, inexpensive materials.

Rarely have I used a program enough to justify a high price tag. Elaborate graphics and educational content are unrelated. I use the money saved to purchase good books. Nonetheless, I make exceptions for solid Catholic material or programs made especially for homeschoolers. Sometimes material published for a small market must be priced higher than that which is mass produced. If the content is superior, the difference in price is worthwhile.

As my children continued growing, I tried something new. Instead of planning the third-grade curriculum in advance, I bought only a basic math book, a catechism, and quality literature reprinted by Bethlehem Books. It was fortunate that I saved the money because later in the year a friend showed me the *Catholic National Readers*, which she had purchased from Kolbe Academy. Readers from this set are now my son's favorite books. I also discovered *Catholic Stories for Boys and Girls*, a marvelous collection reprinted by Neumann Press.

Third grade was a welcome transition. My son became ready for more written work and was able to concentrate for longer periods of time. He slowly changed from a restless young boy to a student capable of sustained work. This transformation led me to appreciate homeschooling all the more. I had waited for my son to indicate signs of readiness, and when he showed the maturity necessary for formal schoolwork, he was not held back by temporary obstacles. We addressed the rough spots and then moved on.

I too have undergone a transformation. My knowledge and experience have increased, and I am confident in my ability to determine what works and what does not work for our family. I can now answer questions as they arise and lead a child on to a higher level of understanding. I also have a house full of wonderful books that I have accumulated through the years. Our learning occurs in many different ways, through planned work in texts, through enriching field trips, and through spontaneous interests.

My children are reaping the benefit of my experience. While teaching my firstborn, I also received a good education. Over the years, we have become a true home-educating family. Our family has found its niche: that niche is home education.

Education commences at the mother's knee, and every word spoken within the hearsay of little children tends towards the formation of character.

—Hosea Ballou, *MS. Sermons.*

Entering God's Boot Camp:
Our First Year
Julie McCaskill

If motherhood is truly the oldest profession, then home-schooling must be the second oldest. While society has lots of how-to advice for being a successful career mother, there is comparatively little available for the aspiring home-schooling mom. To date, I have not seen a book or article that gives any idea about what to expect that first year.

So, let me share with you my top five blunders and my top five blessings. Yes, we all do graduate from boot camp eventually, and then the rest is up to God's loving plan.

We once saw a homeschooler featured on a television news show but did not give the idea a second thought. Later, we began looking into homeschooling at the sugges-tion of a friend whose niece was being homeschooled. At first, I was more for it than my husband; later his enthusi-asm exceeded mine. We were the original teeter-totter couple. But we prayed for direction and when we were faced with a situation that could not be overlooked, we decided that now was the time for action.

Being total and complete novices, we got our packaged curriculum, looked over the material, made up a schedule, bought a globe, and thought that we were ready. We saw homeschooling as a model; you follow the instructions, fit the pieces together, and get the finished product. We never anticipated what would await us when we began home-schooling an eighth-grader who had always been in a traditional parochial school setting. I never realized that this is not something you do but rather a way of life. To date, this has been one of the most profound experiences I have ever had, second only to giving birth.

In the hope that my mistakes will help you, or at least give you a good laugh, I share with you my top five blunders. . . .

Number One: Mom with a mission, or how to drive everyone nuts. Okay, I had my little green binder with all those assignments for the day. This should be routine work, right? Just go through it, complete it, and cross it off, pretty easy. At this point, I equated a good day as one in which we whipped through those assignments without a hitch and a bad day as one where we ended up doing English grammar all day. I have since learned to relax and enjoy the process and not worry about doing everything on schedule. When we began, our daughter had no idea what the capitals of the states were or even all the states' names. Needless to say, there were many other little surprises in store for us. You too may be in for a shock when you find all the gaps in your child's education.

Number Two: House berserk, or role-transition mania. I had been working outside of the home most of my adult life and never knew how to run a house. We used a house-cleaning service, we ate out often, and most of our clothing was drycleaned. Get the picture? I honestly had no idea what stay-at-home moms did all day. I had to learn how to manage a house and how to live on one income instead of two. To those who have never run a household before, I suggest some serious preparation. My favorite books are *Confessions of an Organized Homemaker* and *Confessions of an Organized Family*. They are available at the public library. Additionally, you should develop a budget with your spouse and make a commitment to stick to it. Nothing dampens homeschooling like financial chaos!

Number Three: You are trying to make me a nun. You cannot expect a thirteen-year-old who has attended Mass only on Sunday and prayed only at meals and bedtime suddenly to jump right into daily Mass, Rosaries, Chaplets, and the like, without meeting serious opposition. In our case, we found that it was due to a lack of proper religious instruction and negative peer pressure. Once the Christ-centered curriculum became the norm and religion was being taught daily (not to mention lots of prayer on our part), things did turn around. We still do not make daily Mass together, but we attend several times during the week. Devotions are being added bit by bit with good response. It turns out that slow and steady spiritual progress is better.

Number Four: The search for schedule perfection. Initially, I thought that if I could find the right schedule, everything would be wonderful. Just like finding the right instruction sheet for your model. Now, however, we begin with a general schedule plan for the week and adjust it as needs arise. You do not know what your child knows until you begin. Flexibility is essential. In the beginning, I made my daughter miserable while trying to get her to fit my agenda. I have come to the conclusion that there is no such thing as a perfect schedule. I have also learned that there is no such thing as a normal day. Every day is unique. One day, in utter frustration over the lack of progress in meeting our schedule, I suddenly realized that if the only thing she learned about this year was her faith, that would be the biggest accomplishment in her entire life. After being given that insight (it truly must have come from the Holy Spirit) as to what progress and success are, I relaxed a lot.

Number Five: Do as I say, not as I do. You will find that
what goes around comes around. You cannot expect your
child to demonstrate virtues that you do not yourself demonstrate, especially when that child is a teenager. Your
every defect will be mirrored back to you through your
child and even magnified in the home setting. After all, you
are together all day, every day. With my daughter knowing
that Mom is not perfect, we now work on virtues jointly.
This truly is the Lord's boot camp.

Having discussed the top five pitfalls for homeschooling
rookies, we can now examine the top five blessings of this
great adventure. . . .

Number One: You will get to know your children. You will
learn their strengths, their weaknesses, how they learn
best, when they learn best, and a host of other little items.
Most of all, you will learn how to reach their hearts.

Number Two: You will learn and appreciate your own faith. I
feel like a kid at the ice-cream parlor: so many choices. We
have such an incredible wealth from which to draw in
teaching our children the faith: two thousand years of
Catholic Christian culture, the saints, the history, the
tradition, the art. What an exciting opportunity! This is
not some boring exercise either. For instance, in art, our
daughter was introduced to Fra Angelico's paintings of the
Blessed Mother. She saw that as the artist grew in his
spiritual journey, his paintings became even more beautiful. Our souls too can become more beautiful as we grow in
and practice our faith.

*Number Three: If you did not have a good prayer life before, you
certainly will now.* Nothing brings you to your knees like
your children. I cannot begin to tell you what homeschooling has done for my prayer life, let alone my relation-

ship with our Lord and his Blessed Mother. I could not have survived even one term without adoration of the Blessed Sacrament, the Rosary, daily Bible study, and other spiritual reading, coupled with heartfelt prayer. You are not alone, never ever. The same Lord who gave you your children will give you the graces to teach them what is truly important.

Number Four: Your marriage relationship can and will change. I have received the added gift of better communication with my husband. When a couple is united in achieving a common goal, namely, the education and sanctification of their child, they have a lot to talk about. I quickly learned how important it is to give Dad a daily update on the events of the day. It is amazing how accountability works.

Number Five: You will meet godly women. I had no idea that there was such a great number of truly committed Catholics. They have been an inspiration to me.

Homeschooling is definitely a journey and not a destination to be arrived at. It is a way of life, not something that can be put on and off like a jacket. In the beginning, it feels like boot camp—boot camp sometimes in the desert, or in the swamp, or in the mountains—but always boot camp, where rookies are turned into pros. There are issues we are yet working out, but best of all, God is in charge of the camp. He is able to make good come from mistakes and to put into our life the people who will help us to fill in the areas where we are lacking.

A Dad's Perspective
Richard Wheat

I have to admit, I have it easy. Being the dad in a home-school family, I get up in the morning and help get the kids dressed. Then I escape to the world of work. For nine grueling hours (grueling for my wife, that is), I deal with the daily grind. I thank God that while I am away, my children are with their mother full-time. I am doubly thankful that my wife is willing to undertake the job of homeschooling, which is no small endeavor.

When I return home, the food is on the table—unless it is dance class night, or prayer group night, or one of a thousand other social activities my children are involved in; the kids are bathed; and everything is in order; okay, maybe I am stretching it here. I am basically oblivious to the things that my children do during the day. In this regard, I am like almost every other breadwinner. I am, however, involved in the children's education during my time at home, since learning is an ongoing process.

I find it ironic that parents are often advised to be active participants in their children's education. They are told to look into their local public and private schools, so they can make the best decision for their children. However, should a parent choose to become involved in the actual educa-tion, in the actual teaching, that parent is thought to be on the fringe.

Well, we like the fringe. By homeschooling we not only have the active participation of both parents, but also the knowledge that our children are being taught meaningful information. We avoid the burned-out teachers who are hanging in there for another year before retirement. We avoid the new teacher who wants to experiment with a technique picked up in the last class taken before being certified. We avoid having our child be the thirty-first or thirty-second child jammed into an already overcrowded classroom.

Another benefit is our ability to meet our children's individual needs. I am a firm believer that each child is one of a kind and learns in a unique manner. For some children, a public school setting works well. Other youngsters need the structure and discipline of a private school. I believe we are blessed to have the ability and the desire to homeschool. While this will not work for every child, I am pleased to live in a time when we do not have to go underground to provide what we believe is the best alternative for our children.

I have to admit that sending the children to a public school would be an easy thing to do. No one would question my sanity, nor would they think it improper for me to leave my son at the schoolhouse door. By home-schooling, we are inadvertently sending a message that traditional education is not for everyone. I do not want my family to be cheered or jeered for our decision, but every-one who has seriously discussed homeschooling with a colleague or friend knows it is bound to happen. There is that look that one gets when someone replies, "Ohhh, you homeschoooooool." With the roll of their eyes, they step back a fraction of an inch and judge you.

It is too bad this happens. Fortunately, not everyone is like that. My wife and I have been blessed with meeting so many normal people who homeschool their children. In fact, it was rather shocking to know the vast number of parents who choose this form of education for their family. Homeschoolers are a diverse group and come from all walks of life. I am glad to be a part of this group.

When I get home at the end of a hectic day of work, I know where my children have been, and I know how well they are doing in school. In the evenings and on the weekends, I do my part in enhancing the skills they are learning to master in the classroom. And, personally, I like scheduling the parent-teacher conferences!

We need to believe in the greatness of the American people and the greatness of our families.

—Dan Quayle

Making a List and Checking It Twice

Maureen Wittmann

Some time ago a friend asked me, "What one piece of advice would you give to a new home educator like me?" I answered, "Make a list and find a good support group. Your list should include the reasons why you choose home-schooling for your family. Keep your list handy and refer to it often. Every time you feel discouraged or overwhelmed, pull it out and look it over. You won't believe how much this little routine will help you."

I was speaking from experience. My first year as a home-schooling mother tested the full range of emotions within me. I cannot begin to express the joy I felt when I saw my son grasp a new concept. I could almost see the little lightbulb go on above his head. Yet at the same time, I cannot begin to express the disappointment I experienced when he struggled with something I thought should be a simple task.

I was determined to be the perfect teacher. We seemed to be living in a glass house, as several of my friends and relatives did not support our endeavor. Not only would I prove to them that I could teach my five-year-old son, Christian, but I would also show that he could outperform every single child his age in every single subject. I was setting myself up for failure, and I found myself referring to my list often.

One day was so frustrating that even my list did not help. It was March, and I had been working with my son on phonics since September. We were not getting anywhere;

in fact, it was like pulling teeth. This particular day, he suddenly forgot the sound that the letter "A" makes. It was the first sound he had learned. He had known it the day before, and he had known it six months ago, but somehow it had disappeared from his brain. I convinced myself that it was time to find a private or parochial school, and I began circling choices in the yellow pages. My guardian angel must have flown over to the house of a friend from my homeschool group (Rachel, the co-editor of this book) and whispered in her ear to call.

Just as I was ranting, "That's it! I can't do this; I'm a complete failure; my son can't learn; I can't teach; I'm sending him off to school; let someone else deal with this kid", the phone rang. I began the rant again, this time into Rachel's ear. She calmly pointed out that Christian was only in kindergarten and that he was only five years old. She suggested I relax a bit. She told me that her son, whom I knew to be an avid reader, had struggled at this age as well. She advised that some kids are not ready for reading until as late as eight or nine. She also pointed out that Christian was excelling in his other subjects. We knew he was bright. Perhaps he needed more time on this one.

After the phone call, I pulled out my now-tattered list, and I started to feel better. When I calmed down and thought about the situation, I realized that waiting for my son to develop readiness was a good idea. I checked out the Moores' book *Better Late Than Early*, and we put phonics aside for the year.

Has my son, now seven, learned to read? Well, we are working on it. We changed programs and began using *Teach Your Child to Read in 100 Easy Lessons*. Instead of teaching all of the phonetic sounds first, it introduces a few sounds at a time. This allows the child to begin putting words together immediately. This program, coupled with *Bob Books* and *Little Stories for Little Folks*, has him excited about reading. He is also encouraged by the competition of learning beside his five-year-old sister, Mary.

Putting my reasons for homeschooling on paper and support from my homeschool group got me through my first year. It is smooth sailing now, with just a small bump here and there!

Below is my list as it stands now. It has evolved over several years, and I am sure that it will continue to grow. When you make your own list, remember to keep your reasons positive.

Why We Choose Homeschooling

— To center our lives on the family rather than on school.
— To nurture, train, and educate our children.
— To pass on our faith and culture.
— To foster emotional security.
— To hold our children close while they are young and then let them fly.
— To provide role models ourselves.
— To protect our children from pressure to try drugs or engage in sexual activity before marriage.
— To ensure that the children learn to read phonetically.
— To encourage creativity.
— To provide a classical education.
— To reeducate myself.

Also Because . . .

— We can accomplish more in less time.
— We can vacation and travel during the off-season.

— Socialization, socialization, socialization.
— We can take field trips on the spur of the moment and many of them.
— The Church teaches us that, as parents, we are our children's primary teachers.
— Every child is unique and learns in different ways.
— We know exactly what our children are taught.
— One-on-one tutoring far outweighs large-class settings.
— In this computer age, resources for home educators are bountiful.
— School is in session year round, even on sick days and snow days.
— I love being with my children.

Do not lay up for yourselves treasures on earth, where moth and rust consume, and where thieves break in and steal; but lay up for yourselves treasures in heaven.

—Matthew 6:19–20a

Chapter 2

Sharing Our Philosophies

I have gained from philosophy: that I do without being commanded what others do only through fear of the law.

—Aristotle

Thoughts on Beginning
Home Education
Rachel Mackson

Families approach child discipline in various ways quite successfully. Home education is no different. Be careful not to take any one person's suggestions so seriously that you lose sight of what works for you and your family.

There is always more than one way to get a project done, more than one path to reach the same goal. Let us say that you want to teach reading. If you are new to the prospect, you will likely feel secure starting with a packaged reading curriculum. After teaching your first child, you normally become comfortable using less formal techniques. You might even start improvising, seizing opportune moments as they arise. "What, me?" you say. Yes, you! All you need to feel comfortable is a bit of experience.

Do not worry about ruining your child academically (one of the biggest fears of new home educators). Regular schools teach a spiral curriculum, which means that teachers repeat important information many times over the years. You will make a few mistakes as a new homeschool teacher—all do. Nonetheless, your children will learn and thrive. Why? Because you, like all caring parents, possess a thinking brain. You have the ability to seek out ways and means to educate your own children. It will take initiative and commitment—that is a given—but homeschooling is a work of love that brings great joy to a family. Furthermore, your children have fine, developing brains, and as they reach each stage of readiness, they are eager to make sense of the world.

Even the most highly motivated parent may still be anxious. Nervousness is good if it is used as an impetus to get started investigating the options available to a new homeschooler. There are many wonderful resources to help the busy Catholic homeschool mom provide the right stimulus for her children's intellectual and spiritual growth. If you are daunted, remember, you are not alone on your journey. Many have traveled ahead of you; like you, many are just beginning; and many will follow. Connecting with a homeschooling support group is invaluable. You can meet others who share the same goals. Home educators are notorious for recommending their latest favorite book. Do not let that intimidate you. We were once new ourselves, and it took us years to build our libraries and become knowledgeable about homeschooling resources.

Making contact with individual homeschoolers is also advantageous. I met Maureen, the co-editor of this book, through the local Catholic support group. We have learned from each other, and our homeschooling has benefitted. We jokingly refer to our style as "relaxed classical educa- tion with a Charlotte Mason flavor, permeated with a Catholic world view". It is a rather bookish way, which can seem overwhelming at first, but we did not arrive at the style fully formed. I am a convert to the faith, and it took a long time for me to catch up in this realm. Maureen, on the other hand, was blessed with a superb Catholic upbringing but had gaps in other areas. We helped each other fill in our individual deficiencies and now meet on a common ground.

Children's books have been one of our better aids. I looked everywhere for a clear explanation of the Rosary, and there it was in a Saint Joseph picture book. Maureen loves reading ahead in her children's history books. This practice has an additional benefit. When the children see us read their books, they want to read them too. By reading, or at least skimming the children's books, we make them appear exciting. Like child training, whose ultimate purpose is to form the ability and the desire to do good, education is intended to help the child develop the ability to learn and a passion for learning.

As with any other activity, attitude makes the difference. Whatever your reasons for beginning home education, it is essential to be positive. The longer you homeschool, the easier that becomes.

Thus out of small beginnings greater things have been produced by His hand that made all things of nothing.

—William Bradford

Our Homeschooling Pentecost
Lisa Gayle Brown

We have just finished our second year of homeschooling, by the grace of God and by the skin of our teeth. Our first year progressed more smoothly than the second, in terms of both academics and family life. This second year had pockets of focused and rich school experiences, but they were, unfortunately, few and far between. The year was mainly spent trying to nail down a fairly consistent schedule, with no luck. After much prayer and thought, I believe I see the reason for this downward spiral in our home and school environment in the past year: structure, or the lack thereof.

We began homeschooling in the fall of 1995, but we did not pull our children out of our local parish school for any lofty educational reasons. Basically, we did not care for the socialization that they were receiving at the hands of their peers. My husband and I were shocked at the actions and attitudes of the first-grade boys and the level of maturity of the third-grade girls.

Because we had no specific educational ideology, and because we wanted a truly Catholic education for our children, we enrolled the oldest two with Our Lady of the Rosary School (OLRS) in Bardstown, Kentucky. This Roman Catholic curriculum provider is only an hour away from our home, so the children and I made a visit to their office and warehouse to pick up our books. While we were there, the entire office staff stopped their work at noon and came together to pray the Angelus. My children met a wonderful nun and were mesmerized by her black habit and long, long Rosary beads. She was extremely kind to them. I was hooked!

Bringing home the boxes of books felt like Christmas. I went through the suggestions from the staff at OLRS and began to set up our schoolroom, formerly the den. My mother-in-law, after reading the suggestions from the school, bought us statues of the Holy Family and the Sacred Heart of Jesus to furnish our schoolroom. I plowed through the ten or so teacher manuals for two days, putting together a daily lesson plan from the weekly lesson plans provided by OLRS. We began enthusiastically incorporating the Angelus into our daily routine, just as the office staff at OLRS did each day. My father bought two school desks for our schoolroom, and my husband brought home a chalkboard. We were ready to go.

We maintained a structured routine from September to November 1995. We arose at the same time each morning, had breakfast and prayers together, and began our schoolwork. The children complained somewhat about the quality of the books, especially the readers. I knew this was because their former school did not use Catholic readers and those from OLRS were reprints of older books. The children adjusted to this, and we plowed through. Each weekend, I would spend at least four hours with all the teacher manuals around me, mapping out our daily course of study for the upcoming week. As a new homeschooling mom, I felt that I needed to implement every suggestion, exercise, and project in the teacher manuals.

We made it to the end of the quarter and sent in our quarterly tests to OLRS on time. The school requested that I record the children sight-reading and send in the tape, which I did. Initially, I thought this would be difficult, but it turned out to be no problem at all. The children even enjoyed the recording session. Soon after sending off our quarterly papers and tapes, the children caught colds and became ill. With the holidays approaching and the children sick, I made the decision to suspend all book work until after the new year. In hindsight, this turned out to be the greatest mistake of our first year of homeschooling.

During our holiday break, we received the report cards for the children from OLRS. The children received all A's, but my husband and I were beginning to wonder whether grades were necessary. After all, if a homeschooled child does not understand a concept, it can be repeated until mastery is achieved. Hence, all homeschooled children should receive A's. This new thought, coupled with the lack of any structure in our homeschool for several weeks, made the thought of facing that mountain of teacher manuals daunting. In addition, our middle child, a second-grader, was not adjusting to homeschooling as well as his siblings, and his constant complaining about doing school was wearing on me. We settled into a routine of using the books from OLRS, but not the lesson plans, and supplementing with books from the library. I never sent in another quarterly report.

At this time, I began reading more and more about homeschooling and its different ideologies and methods. Unfortunately, my family is the only homeschooling family in our parish. The nearest Catholic homeschool support group is over an hour away from us. I still had no predominant educational ideology, but I was associating with several families in my area who were followers of John Holt and the unschooling, or child-led, learning philosophy. They have influenced me greatly, both positively and negatively. These unschooling friends taught me to relax and allow my children room to discover their own interests, which was a positive adjustment for us. My middle son began memorizing the presidents of the United States, which revealed to me his huge interest in history. My daughter, now eleven, began showing an interest in everything from sewing (help!) to veterinary science to music.

We got together with these friends several times a week, either to play or to do a hands-on activity. We dressed as Shakers and visited Shakertown, which was a wonderful experience for all of us. We have gone on farm tours and zoo trips, picked berries, played baseball, dipped candles, and made Christmas ornaments. My children have made some wonderful friendships in this group. We went through a period of working in our math books, reading a book from the library, and then turning the children loose to follow their own inclinations for the remainder of the day. I will admit, this was easier than plowing through piles of teacher manuals and fighting with a reluctant child to write sentences with his spelling words. I thought that I had found the homeschooling niche for our family.

It was my husband who first began to have doubts about our new schedule, or lack of schedule. While the children were reading books quite often and keeping up with their religion studies and their math skills, we had no other formal schooling. He was concerned that unschooling would lead to gaps in the children's education. The Holy Spirit began leading my husband back toward a structured, Catholic methodology, and he finally confronted me with a choice: put the children back in the parish school or begin a more structured and classical approach to their education.

This, of course, made me extremely angry at first. I like the hands-on approach to education, and I pointed to the interests that the children had shown in history and animals, as well as their close friendships with the other children. He countered by stressing the benefits of a classical education and the obvious educational gaps observed. This was our argument, back and forth, during most of our second year of homeschooling. Finding a balance between a classical education and a child-led learning approach has not been easy. As a consequence, the children are ahead for their grade level in some areas (particularly math and religion) and behind in others (namely, history and science). For example, my six-year-old, who has never been to school, is not reading at the same level as did my older two, who at his age were in the parish school. This is upsetting to my husband.

I do not mean to imply that an unschooling approach is detrimental. On the contrary, I think that giving children the freedom to explore their world, without the benefit of textbooks and age-segregated classrooms, produces broad-minded and liberal thinkers, in the literal sense. However, as someone who has tried to choose between these two different methodologies, structured, classical education versus unstructured unschooling, I can tell you that it is not easy. At least, I find it difficult. I can see the gaps in the children's education, but I also believe that if we stuck with an unstructured, child-led learning atmosphere, these gaps would close themselves before long. At the same time, I can see the enormous benefits of a classical education, particularly in the languages and literature to be studied. I want my children to be broad-minded thinkers, but I also want them to have a love of learning on their own that will last a lifetime. I knew, though, that in order to be able to keep the children at home, I needed to implement more structured school time to satisfy my husband.

As a Catholic Christian woman, I feel enjoined by God to follow my husband's lead (see Eph 5:22–24 and Col 3:18–

19). Thankfully, the Lord began putting people and incidents into my life to help me see that his plan for our children includes a Catholic classical education. We intend to keep the wonderful friendships that we have made in our small unschooling group, but Rick and I are now more confident in our choice of a structured homeschooling environment for our family. We have a mandate from God, as Rick likes to say, and we are more committed and convinced than ever that homeschooling is God's plan for our family.

Our second year of homeschooling has been a Pentecost, of sorts, in that Rick and I have each learned to follow the Father's will for us and, more important, to be able to discern his will for our family. Through many prayers to our Mother Mary and many conversations with older Christian women, I have learned to be humble and obedient to my husband's lead in our lives, even if I initially disagree with him. Rick has learned, I believe, that homeschooling is the Lord's will for our family at this time, especially in light of our political and social circumstances.

We both accept our position as pioneers in the Catholic homeschooling movement in our area and have learned to follow the guidance of the Holy Spirit in our lives. To me, this lesson is more important than a third-grade history lesson, but I will happily supply the latter and know that I am obeying both my husband and my God when I do so.

To know what you prefer instead of humbly saying Amen to what the world tells you you ought to prefer, is to have kept your soul alive.

—Robert Louis Stevenson

At Home with Our Lady of the Rosary

Julie and Mark Stenske

Homeschooling with a curriculum was our first choice for opening our homeschool. We wanted a support team and felt that a Catholic curriculum provider would fill that need. Just as we benefit from the experiences and suggestions of other homeschooling families, we also benefit from the expertise and training of the curriculum developers. For us, this is all part of the philosophy that the parents are responsible for educating their children. Since we are customers of the curriculum provider, they work for us. The parents are still in charge.

We enjoy following a set lesson plan, although we do adjust the plan to fit our schedule and learning styles. For example, we can do lessons every day until done or do all the work for a subject once a week. There are many possibilities. It is not a problem if we are not on schedule with the school; we work at our own pace.

Another advantage to signing up with a homeschool program is having an objective, professional opinion. At times, it is hard for us to judge whether or not the child's work is adequate for the grade. Naturally, we are impressed with the children because we taught them. It is hard for us to know if we are expecting too much or too little. The guidelines, lesson plans, and grading service gives us the reassurance that we need. We find it easier having a lesson plan. We simply follow it, correct the work, and send it in to be graded. Receiving a report in the mail is also a visible sign that we are accomplishing what we set out to do. We are never surprised by the grades because we have been part of the learning process all along.

Since we are not yet knowledgeable in choosing textbooks, a set curriculum is especially good for us. We do not have the desire or time to call publishers and sort through the myriad different styles and philosophies that are available. We like to concentrate on basic math and spelling for the early years and add in reading assignments. The curriculum makes this easy.

A structured method need not confine one's desires or imagination. In fact, we have found it liberating. Our homeschool is still flexible enough to allow us to change emphasis or add materials we are especially interested in. With so many different programs available, we can easily change if our current course of study no longer meets our particular need or desires. After all, it is easier to change curricula than to change school districts!

We are also helped by having a local Catholic support group. We would not have known where to begin without the advice of our fellow Catholic homeschoolers. There are many good providers of Catholic materials. Meeting others who have used the various materials and curricula helped us determine which particular provider best met our goals.

A Catholic support group and our Catholic curriculum provider give us the help we need to make homeschooling a success for our family.

Homeschool Preschool:
Laying the Proper Foundation
Laurie Navar Gill

My eldest child is completing the fourth grade in our homeschool. If you count the brief and perfunctory year of kindergarten we did, I have five years of experience as a homeschooling mom. But it is more accurate to say that I have been educating for twice that long. From the moment I first beheld my daughter in the delivery room and said to her "I am your Mama", I have been teaching her. Homeschooling begins at birth, and it continues as a natural extension of what we have been doing all along. I must confess that it took me several years to appreciate the importance of the preschool years for laying the proper foundation. It is only now that I have a clear picture of what I want to accomplish with my children during these precious years. This picture has been developed through trial and error, for as we all know, parenting is a learn-as-you-go occupation.

My firstborn had my full attention as I introduced her to letters, numbers, and shapes and read to her endlessly. Inevitably, things were different with my secondborn. While she enjoyed plenty of stimulation from her older sister, she did not get as much of Mom, who was trying to get the beds made and the dishes washed, to clear up the clutter and make headway against the constantly growing piles of laundry.

By the time number three was on the way, we were well

into formal lessons with our eldest, trying to manage the chaos created by an active toddler on the loose while Mom was teaching. Number three, our first son, added considerably to the chaos with his boundless energy and his enthusiasm for throwing, kicking, hitting, and taking apart. We have just had our fourth child, and as our family continues to grow, it becomes more and more apparent that either I will lead these preschoolers or they will overwhelm me and completely rule the house. Because I do not want to live in a home where the youngsters are in charge, I have given plenty of thought to what my goals and philosophies are.

In the past, the energy I directed toward preschool was aimed primarily at developing rudimentary academic skills. Yet my homeschooling experience has taught me how easily a child can learn the alphabet, numbers, and all the things found in commercial workbooks when he is developmentally ready. Consequently, I think these years are better spent learning the habits and attitudes without which learning cannot be accomplished: obedience, orderliness, and sincerity. Through beginning to learn these virtues, our children will be more enjoyable as toddlers and preschoolers, they will make less mischief for Mother to clean up, and they will be ready to work when they reach their turn for formal schooling.

I will consider first the virtue of obedience. I cannot claim to be an expert in fostering compliance in children, as I admit that none of mine is perfectly obedient. Yet I will share my thoughts on this most important virtue. Our aim is not simply to have children who do what we say because they have no choice, but rather to foster the will to do what is right. Preschoolers will not know what is right, so parents must have far-sighted vision as they go about instructing these littlest ones.

Some people recommend physically forcing toddlers to obey. I do not see the point of doing so, as it does not in any way train the child's will. Instead, I insist that my little ones obey my voice, and I reprove them if they do not. The key, as we all know, is consistency. Each and every willful act of defiance must be dealt with swiftly and surely. Although a fully formed will does not develop instantly, over time the challenges will be fewer in number. I pray for God's aid in being as consistent as my toddlers require.

I like to use stories to teach, and there are a great many that illustrate the importance of obedience. Two of my favorites are *Mr. Gumpy's Outing*, by John Burningham, and *Strega Nona*, by Tomie de Paola. Both of these are well-illustrated and engaging stories that illuminate the catastrophic consequences of disobedience. In addition, the story of the Ten Commandments can be taught to toddlers as an example of God giving his children rules. For our preschoolers, we emphasize the two great commandments on which, Jesus said, "depend all the law and the prophets" (See Mt 22:34–40). Having family rules is also important. We write ours down so that the children can see them even if they cannot read them.

The next virtue I am seeking to instill is orderliness. If you require preschoolers to put away their own things when they are finished with them, they will learn to be orderly. For children, work can be play; therefore, parents can make tidying up a game. The key is to focus on the process and not on the end result. Orderliness is also fostered by a regular schedule. It can be as flexible as you like, but teaching little ones that every day has its own order will be useful as you move into formal studies.

My favorite books on orderliness include *A Child's Rule of Life*, by Msgr. Robert Hugh Benson, available from

Neumann Press; *The Maggie B.*, by Irene Haas; and *Mrs. Tiggy-Winkle* (and others), by Beatrix Potter. *A Child's Rule* covers a Catholic child's daily schedule. *Maggie B.* and *Mrs. Tiggy-Winkle* are examples of books that make housework seem exciting and grown-up. Mothers might even find themselves inspired. The creation story from the Bible is another good story to use in teaching order.

Finally, I would like to examine sincerity, which for small children means telling the truth. The ability to recognize and value the truth is essential for academic progress. Preschoolers should be helped to distinguish between fantasy and reality and to become reliable reporters. Give them opportunities to retell stories of events that have happened to them and of things they have read. Point out the difference between made-up stories and those that actually occur. My favorite stories for teaching the importance of telling the truth are "The Boy Who Cried Wolf" and "Charley and the Yellow-Jackets" (which is in the "Harvest" chapter of Laura Ingalls Wilder's *Little House in the Big Woods*).

Obedience, orderliness, and sincerity have become the foundation of my preschool curriculum. David Isaacs, in his book *Character Building*, which is available through Seton, discusses these in depth. Reading this book has been a help as I work with my toddlers to obtain these virtues. I have confidence that I will use their developmental abilities to help them become ready learners when the time for school arrives. Moreover, it is my fervent prayer that helping my little ones in these areas will help me to improve as well.

The Early Elementary Years
Rachel Mackson

The early elementary years have been called by Dorothy Sayers the Poll Parrot stage. Children of this age thrive on rhythmic language and memorize information rather effortlessly. I can remember when my babies were about two years old. They would say something rather advanced for their age. At first, I would be impressed, then I would realize they did not understand the words. They were simply imitating my speech patterns by repeating a sentence I had spoken earlier.

This ability to absorb and imitate is inborn. Think of how little children love to repeat words from their favorite songs, movies, and books. In the same manner, our school-age children retain this love of rhythmic language and repetitions. As we begin homeschooling, we can tap this reservoir. There is nothing at all wrong, and a lot right, about having children memorize the states and their capitals. Many children enjoy doing so, and many parents enjoy teaching this type of information.

But we can also take advantage of this inborn talent as an opportunity to imprint our children with the beautiful and poetic language of great literature. When we read aloud to children, they effortlessly soak up the broad historical panorama of Western civilization and Church tradition. Instead of just learning math, children can also understand how our number system was developed. They can learn a framework now so that later, when they study topics in depth, they have a way to categorize information.

Building a framework is of utmost importance. So often, we teach children little tidbits of knowledge. We forget that they need help building a filing system so they can correlate and interrelate their learning. We happen to live in the age of data overload. It is therefore critical for our children to develop the ability to evaluate and place new knowledge. If they do not, they may succeed quite well in learning facts without developing the skill necessary to think about all the information sent their way by the modern world.

In her essay "The Lost Tools of Learning" (reprinted in *National Review*, January 19, 1979), Dorothy Sayers speaks to this point: "Is not the great defect of our education today, a defect traceable through all the disquieting symptoms of trouble that I have mentioned, that although we often succeed in teaching our pupils subjects, we fail lamentably on the whole in teaching them how to think?" A few paragraphs later she goes so far as to exclaim, "We who were scandalized when men were sent to fight armored tanks with rifles, are not scandalized when young men and women are sent into the world to fight massed propaganda with a smattering of subjects."

Please do not panic and think you need to abandon subject learning completely in order to follow Miss Sayers' advice. It is possible to follow her advice without deviating drastically from your current ways. Instead of abandoning subjects, combine them or make them transparent to the children. For example, if you read aloud from a wonderful little book on the story of numbers, are the children learning history or math? Is retelling a passage from a book reading comprehension or oral speaking? I say all of the above, plus thinking skills.

So, specific subjects are important. We often do study them. Still, in the early elementary years, we should also pay attention to erecting a broad and rich foundation upon which the children can build as they mature and are able to study more independently. I think of it as establishing a thirst for truth and knowledge and an enjoyment of things of the mind.

As Charlotte Mason, a well-known educator from the nineteenth century would say, "Expose the children to a broad range of noble and lofty ideas." Each child may respond a bit differently, but you can rest assured they will respond. I personally have found that the easiest way to expose my children to a broad range of ideas is to read books aloud to them. It seems basic, yet it is vital for learning. Turning my children on to good books has been a big step forward to successful homeschooling.

How did I accomplish this goal? I began with one book. I sat down and started reading. It was that simple. Soon, I was surrounded by curious children. When I began to read out loud, I gathered quite a following and utilized this to my best advantage by alternating great fiction with more informative selections. Although my littlest ones did not stick around as long as the older children, they learned a great deal as they played without appearing to listen.

I am a busy homeschooling mom, with toddlers and nursing babies ever demanding my attention. I have only so much time. Yet I consider the intervals spent reading aloud from a broad range of good fiction and non-fiction to be one of the most important homeschool techniques at my disposal. It is the best a lecture could be and is an exceptional way to impart knowledge.

As great as reading aloud is, children eventually become capable of reading for meaning on their own. When independent reading improves, the ability to learn expands. During the transition, as independent reading grows, I introduce a new subject by reading from a book. After an interest is sparked, the children continue on their own. For this reason, stocking a home library is essential.

As long as you feed your children the proper spiritual and intellectual food, education in the early elementary years will be a success. Moreover, the most rewarding aspect of homeschooling is watching the children learn and grow, knowing their hearts and souls are being well nourished in the bosom of their family, and knowing they are receiving the proper foundation now for future growth.

The direction in which education starts a man will determine his future life.

—Plato, *The Republic*

Unschooling for a Change

Karen Urness

It is a Thursday afternoon, and I look around our small home at my five children. Kelly, age thirteen, works confidently in her algebra book. Completing her second math book this year has been her goal. Our twelve-year-old son, Sean, is busily drawing in his sketch book. Looking over his shoulder, I am amazed at the quality of his drawings. Ten-year-old Ryan, snuggled up on my bed, is reading the biography of Thomas Jefferson. Molly, age seven, busies herself with the microscope. She is examining her mother's blood (ouch!) on a slide. Erin, age two, has four puzzles in progress on the living room floor.

Chaos? I do not think so. We have begun the process of unschooling. This has been a journey for me that has not come easily. Prior to our more relaxed approach, I used a prepared curriculum, worksheets, and tests. The children and I spent hours each day at the kitchen table poring over workbook questions, math equations, and reports. For seven years this formal method worked well for us, or so I thought. At times, the days would drag on. After a while, weeks would become mundane. The children were tired of the ritual, and so was I. We plodded on, and sometime after my fifth child, Erin, was born this schedule began to take its toll on me and on the children. My usually complacent bunch was rebelling. They were becoming lazy and stagnant, and they were beginning to hate learning. They were also becoming a discipline problem and squabbled frequently over little things. I was getting resentful of their intrusion in my life. In short, I was considering putting them in school.

After I shared my displeasure with a friend, she suggested unschooling. She explained unschooling as learning that is led by the child. This idea was unfamiliar to me, and I was apprehensive about its outcome. To get me started, my friend suggested that I do absolutely nothing in the way of formal lessons for six weeks. I was alarmed at first, but agreed to try it. It was, I think, a type of detox. I was concerned that the children would vegetate and become even lazier than usual. She assured me that this would not happen, and we began the next day.

The first week my children walked around the house in a daze. They had no direction and did not know what to do with themselves. Of course, they begged for television, but I refused.

The second week was spent outdoors, and the children began to investigate our wooded backyard. I noticed the fighting and whining subsiding in favor of camaraderie and laughter. After a day or two of investigating, the children began to drag piles of wood to the backyard. Tools were worn on their belts and gloves on their hands. "What are you up to?" I probed. "We're building a fort", Sean replied. I chuckled to myself and wondered what four young kids could do with wood, a few tools, and no experience at all. Resisting the temptation to interfere, I went on with my housework and tended to the baby. After some time, Ryan waltzed in and requested that we drive to the library to get books on building forts. I was thrilled by this request, and we all raced to the van!

At the library, I watched as the children went to the computer to look up the topic, wrote down the call numbers, and searched the shelves to see what they could find.

We left the library with twenty-two books on woodworking and building forts, houses, playgrounds, doll houses, etc.

After deciding on a plan, the children wrote out their diagram on a piece of paper. They made careful measurements and went to work. They spent weeks on the project, digging a basement, building a floor, and devising a pulley system to raise and lower supplies. Despite all of their efforts, the task was a difficult one and is still in progress. They hope to complete their building this summer.

The children worked on the fort themselves with no unsolicited help from me or my husband. We were there for assistance and direction, but the core of the project was theirs alone. In spite of my original skepticism, the children were learning this unschooling way. While the design unfolded, they practiced many subjects, including reading, writing, drafting, math, woodworking, social interaction, computer use, and research skills.

Now, what if we attempted unschooling for the remainder of our year? What would happen? First, the children began to search for pen pals and in the process learned more writing skills. Second, the parents abandoned most of their formal schooling ideas and let the children lead the way.

Still wanting to nudge them in certain directions, I suggested that they investigate jobs they might like when they became adults. This idea intrigued them, and after looking into careers, they now want to learn the subjects that they will need for high school and college. For example, my eldest is interested in becoming an accountant. She is working diligently on her math skills. The other children are exploring alternative directions and are full of excitement and curiosity.

They are focusing on topics of their choosing, and the subjects they are learning make a larger impact on their lives than they would if I were preparing a schedule for them. When faced with the thought that I should go back to a more strict schedule, I remember my elementary, secondary, and college years. The subjects that I remember best are the ones in which I was most interested. When the children are leading the way, they have greater retention.

At times I do prompt their learning. We have lots of books in our home for the children to read. Often, when I find a new topic that I would like the children to learn, I leave the appropriate books lying around the house for them to investigate. Frequently, this is all that they need to become interested. If the interest is not present, I put the book on the shelf for a while.

Spending vast quantities of time outdoors is quite effective for encouraging learning. Daily walks open our life to trees, flowers, insects, and wildlife. Walks are a wonderful introduction to nature and prompt additional research. The simple act of picking up stray rocks often causes a flurry of interest in geology. Gardening introduces several subjects: botany, physical education, reading, and math skills. Few things are as rewarding to a youngster as preparing a garden bed. The feel of the soil filling the spaces between their little fingers, planting, and watering the seeds provide interest to a young child. It all leads to the pleasure of watching their seedlings grow into scrumptious vegetables or breathtaking flowers.

We make certain to limit their television to appropriate channels. The Public Broadcasting Service, nature, and science channels are especially helpful in getting the creative spark ignited. We also have many educational board games and computer games available. The new geography games are especially helpful. The children have a better knowledge of geographical locations than I had at their age.

At times I still wonder whether I am on the right track with my children's education. Stepping back, I notice that much of the whining and squabbling has abated. The children retain more than they did previously. They are learning in a style that suits them as well as me. We enjoy reduced pressure to conform to school schedules. The children are able to spend more time with music and other activities. I also enjoy more time for myself. Unschooling allows me the freedom to pursue hobbies of my own choosing, such as music and writing. Will I ever return to my old ways? I doubt it.

For more information on unschooling, Home Education Magazine (HEM) *is a good resource. Their offices can be contacted at (800) 236-3278 or HomeEdMag@aol.com. You receive a free sample issue upon request. Please keep in mind that* HEM *is a secular magazine.*

He will feed his flock like a shepherd, he will gather the lambs in his arms, he will carry them in his bosom, and gently lead those that are with young.

—Isaiah 40:11

Battling Burnout
Cindy Garrison

This past year we finally found a workable way to schedule our school year that made us all happy. During the first two years of homeschooling, I worked outside our home two days a week. We began by doing schoolwork on weekends to make up for these two days, but we did not care for that schedule. We then started doing extra work in the more critical subjects, such as religion, math, English, and phonics, on the days I was home. In the evenings of my work days, we spent about one-and-a-half hours working on the other subjects. This schedule was better for us.

The first year we continued right through the summer and began again in September. We took a couple of weeks off here or there, depending on our holiday or vacation schedule. By the end of the second year, we were all burned-out and took the summer months off.

When we started again in September, both my fourth-grade daughter, Ashley, and I were disappointed to realize how much she had forgotten over the summer. She had worked hard memorizing her multiplication tables, but by neglecting them during the summer she had forgotten most of them. We spent four weeks of that school year in review. I decided there must be a better way. I asked God to help show me what that way might be.

We finished our third school year at the end of the second week in May. We took the last two weeks of May off. I was able to spend those two weeks preparing lesson plans, since I had already purchased the kids' curriculum for the next year.

We began our fourth year in June. We schooled for two weeks, then took the last two weeks of each summer month off: June, July, and August. From September to December we schooled three weeks and took off the last week of each month. In January, we reversed the schedule to get a two-week Christmas break. From January to June we took off the first week of each month and schooled the last three weeks.

This schedule was just what our family needed. Everyone worked hard during the weeks we schooled because we knew a break would come soon. During the week off, we tried to do some of the things we might not ordinarily do during a school week, such as taking a field trip or visiting far-away relatives. Everyone seemed happier, and we did not experience the burnout we had in the past.

Our fifth year of homeschooling has begun, and it is such a joy to hear words of excitement when the books arrive, instead of words of dread. We will continue this year with the same schedule as last year and thank God that he showed us a way that works well for us.

I encourage anyone who is feeling burned-out or looking for a better way to set up the school year to keep trying different schedules until you find what works for your family. Always trust in God and ask him for guidance. He will lead you down the right path.

The world is so full of a number of things,
I'm sure we should all be as happy as Kings.

—Robert Louis Stevenson

What Is Classical Education?

Rachel Mackson

Discussions of classical education are usually peppered with mysterious-sounding terms: the liberal arts, the trivium, the quadrivium, and "lost tools". This often causes confusion.

Upon investigation, however, things turn out to be not so mysterious. Like many words in our English language, *liberal arts*, *trivium*, and *quadrivium* come from Latin, although many of the ideas behind the words come from the Greeks. The ancient world was composed of free men and slaves, and work was divided accordingly. The Latin *liberalis* means "suitable for freemen", and *ars* means "knowledge or skill". Thus we see that the liberal arts refer to the knowledge suitable for study by free men, as opposed to the drudgery fit for slaves.

After the fall of Rome, education was preserved by the Church and was kept alive in the monasteries and later in the universities. It is this religious model that holds the most interest for me. As a Catholic homeschooler, I am looking for pedagogical models that interweave religious training and high academic ideals. The Church used classical education as the means to sharpen the mind to know, love, and serve God better and to give order to an often chaotic world. Latin was the language of the educated and of the Church. Religion formed the basis of all studies, but men subdivided learning into the seven liberal arts: grammar, rhetoric, dialectic (logic), geometry, arithmetic, astronomy, and music. They further split this array of seven into a group of three verbal arts called the trivium, after the Latin *tri* for "three" and *via* for "way", and a group of four mathematical arts called the quadrivium, after the Latin *quad* for "four". The trivium—grammar, rhetoric, and dialectic (logic)—was considered the foundation for study of the quadrivium—geometry, arithmetic, astronomy, and music. Today, it is not inconsistent with this model to study arts other than music, or science other than astronomy.

The lost tools were not difficult to locate. I found them in an essay by Dorothy Sayers, "The Lost Tools of Learning" (reprinted in *National Review*, January 19, 1979). Modern education, according to Miss Sayers, leaves students sorely lacking in the tools necessary to be independent learners and thinkers. Children are taught a broad variety of subjects but are not given adequate educational footing. Proper study of the three disciplines leaves a student well equipped with the tools of language, persuasive communication, and reason within a framework of religious training. Miss Sayers' essay piqued my interest, and a friend, Patsy Conley, lent me *The Seven Liberal Arts in the Middle Ages*, by David Wagner. I delved deeper into the topic.

In the early years of medieval classical education, grammar held primacy. Memorization is important for this study but is by no means the whole. To learn the grammar of a language, scholars need to memorize unfamiliar vocabulary and understand how the words relate. In medieval times, students focused on Latin exclusively. No one bothered with formal study of his native language. Greek is considered a more elegant language than Latin, and much of the early writings of our Western civilization are in Greek, so a true classical education includes both languages. Catholic homeschoolers typically focus on English grammar and Latin. Why Latin? Because it is the language of the Church and because it lays the groundwork for many Western languages. Learn Latin first, and you have one of the keys to English and the family of Romance languages.

Literature study is included under the grammar heading. Pupils read the classic literature of Western civilization and of the Church. Their minds are expanded by planned exposure to the intellectual giants. Instead of reading summaries, students read original texts and think deeply about them. Here, grammar and logic overlap. Students are expected to read reflectively, examining underlying assumptions and looking for inconsistencies in logic. In the homeschool, study of grammar, systematic study of an ancient language, and reading good literature leave pupils equipped with a firm command of the fundamentals of language and the confidence to tackle other subjects. Most home educators include the classics of all ages, ancient through modern.

Saint Augustine promoted the study of pagan rhetoric in his book *De doctrina christiana* so that Christians could defend their faith against others. He felt that eloquence was learned through imitation rather than wisdom. As students mature and learn to apply logic, their ability to communicate thoughts and ideas expands. Students begin by studying the techniques of great orators and writers of the past, and in the end, find the style that works best for them. Rigorous study of rhetoric hones the ability to write and speak effectively. It is not enough to think great thoughts; one must also be able to explain those thoughts to others.

The next area of study, the dialectic, regained its position of distinction in the trivium through the work of

Gerbert, the leading scholar of the tenth century. His influence was great because he later became Pope Sylvester II. The dialectic, before Gerbert's time, emphasized reasoning that persuades as opposed to deductive reason that is self-evidently true, a subtle difference. Here again, there is overlap among the liberal arts. Dialectic is a verbal logic akin to apologetics. Deductive reasoning, however, is formal mathematical logic and is studied under geometry. Both are important. Students are expected to do more than absorb information; they are expected to begin critiquing and relating all subjects. Instead of being split apart, studies need to be interrelated. Individual topics are properly understood only in a broader context. Pupils learn to make connections and evaluate new information in light of the values they already possess. Then they are ready to go a step farther and argue persuasively. Clear reasoning is the goal of dialectic and logic.

In modern times, classical educators often simplify the divisions of the trivium to grammar, logic, and rhetoric. Such groupings are not inconsistent, because there is an essential unity to the trivium and to the liberal arts as a whole: you read (grammar); you analyze (logic); and you defend, explain, or teach (rhetoric). If you look closely, you will spot reading, 'riting, and 'rithmetic on this list.

Now I understood why Miss Sayers spoke of lost tools: grammar gives students a firm command of language; rhetoric promotes eloquent expression; and dialectic (logic) exercises the ability to reason. Such a foundation under the guidance of religious and moral formation equips a student with the ability to learn any subject, communicate articulately in written and oral form, and think logically. As David Wagner stated in *The Seven Liberal Arts*, students gain "knowledge of the divine and the power to express it".

These lofty ideals of study look beautiful on paper, but I wondered if it was possible to accomplish them in the homeschool. The answer is a resounding yes. Throughout their years of living and growing together, children and parents can live and study the Catholic faith. The youngest of children can study grammar through the memorization of prayers in English and Latin. As the children mature, Latin and Greek studies can begin. When children reach their argumentative stage, one can give them meaty topics to worry about and encourage them to reason persuasively about controversial issues of the day. Around the age of ten or twelve, they can begin the study of formal logic. Finally, in the high school years, homeschooling children can study rhetoric systematically so they can mature into adults capable of articulating and defending their ideals.

There are many resources to help homeschooling families incorporate classical education into their home studies. Laura Berquist's *Designing Your Own Classical Curriculum* is an excellent start for those wanting to create their own program. She has founded the Mother of Divine Grace Independent Study Program. Another school, Kolbe Academy, offers structured support to homeschoolers by providing syllabi, help in choosing texts, and phone consultations. Kolbe also offers a well-chosen selection of books for sale to individuals. Last on my list, but not last in helpfulness, is Regina Coeli Online Academy, which presents classes via computer, thereby connecting homeschoolers with a wide range of teachers and students.

Saint Thomas Aquinas thought the liberal arts prepared men for philosophy, whose chief concerns were God and the soul. Although I am not a classical-education purist by any stretch of the imagination, my investigations have yielded many fruits, not the least of which is a richer depth

of understanding. Adding classical elements to our academic pursuits has provided a better education for all the
members of our family.

But one cannot live on capital forever. However firmly a tradition is rooted, if it is never watered, though it dies hard, yet in
the end it dies. And today a great number—perhaps the majority—of the men and women who handle our affairs, write our
books and our newspapers, carry out our research, present our
plays and our films, speak from our platforms and pulpits—yes,
and who educate our young people—have never, even in a
lingering traditional memory, undergone the Scholastic discipline.

—Dorothy L. Sayers

Chapter 3

Resources
for Basic Subjects

And they devoted themselves to the apostles' teachings and fellowship, to the breaking of bread and the prayers.

—Acts 2:42

Teaching the Faith
Patsy Conley

The best way that I have found to teach the faith to my five children is to live it with them. We attend Mass as often as possible during the week, celebrate the liturgical year in our home, and stock our personal library with Catholic books. Bringing the Faith fully into the home as daily routine is a great way to impart the Faith to children. The rest is fine tuning. For this reason I begin with a list of resources for parents.

Inspiration for living the liturgical year of the Church can be found in Ecclesiastes, in the first part of chapter three. We learn that there is a time to fast and a time to feast; a time to mourn and a time to rejoice. The celebration of the liturgical year not only helps establish these times but also helps bring the life of Church liturgy into the home, thus making a strong connection between the two.

Home education allows parents to lead their family to faith in great abundance. It also allows parents the freedom to devote time to special seasons of the Church. For example, home educators can schedule a week or two of cookie baking during the Advent season, discussing the historical significance of each recipe (see *A Continual Feast*, below).

On the following pages, I give two lists—first, a list of books that are helpful to parents in imparting the Faith to their children, and second, a list of books that are intended for reading by the children.

Resources for Parents

Catholic Traditions in Crafts
Ann Ball, available from Our Sunday Visitor

This is the only book currently in print with detailed, colorful directions for crafts relating to the liturgical year. It has projects ranging from the simple to the complex.

Celebrating Advent and Christmas: A Sourcebook for Families
Celebrating Lent and Easter: A Sourcebook for Families
Helen Hull Hitchcock, Women for Faith and Family

These books contain special devotions for Advent, Christmas, Lenten, and Easter activities and recipes. Articles on music, symbolism, and tradition are included.

Celebrating the Faith in the Home series
Teresa Zepada and Laurie Navar Gill, Gilhaus Communications

A delightful series published by two homeschooling mothers. The books are inspirational, practical, and easy to use. When the authors mention making Advent decorations for a Jesse tree, they thoughtfully include patterns.

A Continual Feast
Evelyn Birge Vitz, Ignatius Press

This cookbook lists at least 275 recipes and includes informative historical explanations and tips for baking with children. There are many blessings, graces, and menus for holidays sprinkled throughout.

Expressions of the Catholic Faith, A Guide to the Teachings and Practices of the Catholic Church
Kevin Orlin Johnson, Ph.D., Ballantine Books

This book is an excellent resource, giving the historical symbolism underlying many traditional practices. The historical development of the stations of the cross and the logic behind them, reasons behind the use of candles in prayer and liturgy, and even a surprising story of Christianity's best-known symbol, the sign of the cross, are all found. I have mentioned only a small portion of the content.

Guiding Your Roman Catholic Preschooler
Kathy Pierce and Lori Rowland, Good Catholic Books

Filled with practical tips and resources, including movies, to help you raise your little ones as Catholics.

The Saints and Our Children
Mary Reed Newland, TAN Books

This book delivers far more than you might expect. It is a wonderful aid for Catholic mothers and fathers. In our family, we try to mention many of the saints' feast days, but there are a few that we choose to celebrate with Mass, a substantial family meal, and a discussion of the saints' virtues. Mrs. Newland's books have passed one of the tests of being declared a classic, the test of time.

The Year and Our Children
Mary Reed Newland, Firefly Press

A forty-year-old book cherished by Catholic mothers all over America is newly reprinted. It is a practical guide celebrating the Church year in the home. Written with a mother's insight, it is full of historical and personal anecdotes.

Catholic Books for Children

Catholic National Readers
Rev. Richard Gilmour, D.D., available from Kolbe Academy

For those who like the *McGuffey's Readers* but desire a Catholic perspective. All six levels contain stories that exemplify high morals and are sure to bring warmth to the hearts of all readers both young and old.

Catholic Stories for Boys and Girls
Neumann Press

These stories of courage, charity, and faith were written in the 1930s by nuns. They are heart-warming children's stories; you may need your handkerchief to get through the collection.

Catholic Treasure Box Series
Edited by Maryknoll Sisters, TAN Books

These are colorful, solidly Catholic, picture books that children find delightful.

My Jesus and I
Rev. Louis Laravoire Morrow, available from Seton

This is a prayerbook for young children; its beautiful illustrations are jewels. It is a great generator of discussion.

Saint Joseph Picture Books
Father Lovasik, available from most Catholic bookstores

Father Lovasik's books on the saints and the faith are loved by children. Most are small and inexpensive. My children took apart their *Saint Joseph* book on the stations of the cross and mounted the pictures on cardboard. We used them for home stations during Lent. These books are a valuable resource for any home library.

The Mitchells: Five for Victory
Hilda van Stockum, Bethlehem Books

Bethlehem books has reprinted this delightful book and many others by the same author. The books are humorous and fast-paced, featuring larger families and positive moral values.

Vision series of saints' stories
Ignatius Press

A wonderful series—a delight for young and old.

Every method of education founded, wholly or in part, on the denial or forgetfulness of original sin and of grace, and relying on the sole powers of human nature, is unsound.

—Pope Pius XI: *Divinus Illius Magistri* (December 31, 1929)

Math in the Home
Rachel Mackson

The subject most likely to stump a new home teacher is math. Many parents have memories of math confusion. Furthermore, the conflict over how to teach the subject is just as polarized as the debate about whole language versus phonics. The old argument between the two camps of drill, drill, drill versus understanding is a good example of errors coming into the world in pairs. I do not think it has to be that way. There are many splendid resources. The dazed and confused parent can find clarity.

In many ways, math is like art. You do not want to throw out technique and drill; but then again, you do want your program to include creativity and problem-solving. Appreciating the great works of art and the great mathematical problems is worthwhile. But just as some artists go overboard and focus so much on the creativity that they produce art viewers have difficulty comprehending, some modern math teachers go overboard and focus so much on problem-solving that they forget it is difficult to solve problems without a background of math facts. In contrast, some texts reduce math to small pieces and miss the whole. They have too much technique and not enough creativity or appreciation of the great problems of math. Mathematics is an exciting topic that has all too often been robbed of its splendor.

Teaching math is not much different from teaching history. It appears easier to buy a textbook and go through it chapter by chapter. History could be presented as a bare timeline with dates and names to be memorized. Most homeschoolers, however, put more effort into the subject. They read biographies, do small unit studies, and search out attractive resources. Some completely eliminate a text for extended periods of time and buy a good overview of history to read, thus educating themselves so they can better educate their children.

You can do the same with math. Basic arithmetic and math functions are important to learn, but they are not the entire program. You can add to the arithmetic base by reading biographies, doing unit studies on interesting math topics, displaying posters, and more. Parents can also read to obtain the big picture of math. If you reflect on the subject, before long you will realize how amazing it is that math works. Through the centuries men have detected many naturally occurring patterns, some with practical applications, some without. Once they observed the regularity, men noticed endless repetitions in nature. Some of the first Greek mathematicians made their discoveries when examining the intervals between notes on the musical scales. Thus math began. More recently, modern mathematicians tried to study chaos and found they could not. There was an underlying order imbedded in what at first appeared to be chaos.

I cannot tell anyone exactly how to teach math because there is such a diversity of families educating their children at home. My hope is that I can help people fall in love with math and find the confidence to explore and experiment on their own. Absolutely, please, do not feel that you have to run out and buy all the resources listed. Math is one of my hobbies, so I have accumulated many items through the years. Start small!

If you own a computer, programs are the easiest way to

enliven your math studies. *The Logical Journey of the Zoombinis*, available from Broderbund, covers logic and algebraic thinking yet can be played by a seven-year-old. It is so entrancing that many parents sneak off to play when the kids are not looking. Edmark's latest, the *Mighty Math* programs, are almost a complete math curriculum and are worthy entertainment. Another outstanding line is the *Treasure* series by The Learning Company.

I also consider books to be one of the simplest supplements. *Mathematicians Are People Too* and *Number Stories of Long Ago* are fine additions to our read-aloud time. I also have books accessible for independent browsing by the children. *Story Problems to Solve*, from Dale Seymour, *Understanding Math*, from Reader's Digest, and *Math Smart Junior*, by Princeton Review, are a few titles that come to mind. Usborne also has several appealing books for the younger set.

If you prefer hands-on alternatives, try *Math Wizardry for Kids*, available in most bookstores. It has fun, catchy, math activities. I have had success with *Math Art*, by Creative Teaching Press. It has a variety of educational art projects, ranging from simple cutting and gluing to one-point perspective drawing. I have not used it as much as I would like to—ah, the dreams we have for the perfect homeschool— but the projects we have completed have gone over well. Browsing through your local teacher supply store and through the Dale Seymour and Cuisenaire catalogs will enable you to see what is available. In our household, we have enjoyed the large set of wooden pattern blocks. They have provided hours of play for our children. Cuisenaire rods are fun too, but budget-conscious parents can present the same concept with Lego bricks.

When you feel full of enthusiasm, *Historical Topics for the Mathematics Classroom* will give you invaluable background information for planning a unit study. *Historical Topics* explains math history but is somewhat dry. *Journey through Genius* is easier to read but not as thorough. *Journey* includes full math proofs; but even if you cannot follow the formal presentations, there is still a considerable amount that you can learn from the parts written in plain English. Another book, *Joy of Mathematics*, is wonderful in presenting math in a way that reluctant parents can appreciate. Your local library is also bound to have several books that you can peruse, such as *A History of Mathematics*, by Carl B. Boyer.

If all this sounds complicated, and you only want to add independent work to the daily assignments, *Mathematical History: Activities, Puzzles, Stories, and Games* is a good, inexpensive supplement. Most pages have a historical math story on one side with a related puzzle or game on the other. Our family has also enjoyed *Beginning Algebra Thinking*, by the Ideal School Supply Company.

For fourth grade and up, *The Problem-Solving in Mathematics* series is a well-done work-text, with notes for the teacher included. It is arranged so you can pick topics out of order, making it perfect for doing a short unit. Consider skimming the book with your children to find a section that catches their eye. These workbooks are produced for several grade levels but are flexible enough so that one can be used with several children at a time. Combining *Problem-Solving* with the popular *Key to Math* workbook series provides a complete program that children can use with relative independence.

Another simple-to-implement workbook is *Critical Thinking Activities*, from Dale Seymour. It is a less expensive alternative to the *Building Thinking Skills* series recommended by many in homeschooling circles. It covers the type of thinking often found on IQ and standardized tests and comes with an answer key built in. I include the challenging activities from this book about once every two weeks. I schedule them in because the skills will be useful when the children take the inevitable standardized test. Sometimes I assign pages in a "do-this" manner. But on an occasional Saturday, my husband and I will start doing a problem, and, before we know it, we are surrounded by helpers.

Before closing, I should mention games. Monopoly has lots of basic math, especially for the banker. Games like Parcheesi, Mancala, and backgammon offer young children opportunities to practice thinking strategies and addition. Checkers provides the opportunity for children to plan long-term strategies. Guess Who introduces logic and is playable by children as young as five. Even simple games like Trouble or Chutes and Ladders give counting practice.

Let me finish on this note, so that I do not overwhelm anyone with possibilities: I do not abandon traditional math teaching, but I do enrich our studies. There is more to math than what is included in back-to-basic textbooks, and there are many options for teaching and learning math. If what you are currently doing works, great. If not, start exploring.

For information on the resources mentioned, see Appendix D.

In symbols one observes an advantage in discovery which is greatest when they express the exact nature of a thing briefly and, as it were, picture it; then indeed the labor of thought is wonderfully diminished.

—Gottfried von Leibniz

Effective Spelling Instruction
Beverly L. Adams-Gordon

The most efficient and effective way to teach spelling has been debated for ages. English spelling is particularly difficult because there are 250 ways to spell approximately forty-six sounds in the language. Modern English is a blend of Anglo-Saxon and French, with many words borrowed from other languages. Its spellings can be traced back to the differing practices developed in various regions of England.

Spelling has become one of the most researched aspects of instructional theory. I will review some of the research findings.

Appropriate placement of the individual student is the most important key to effective instruction. Gertrude Hildreth and others conducted studies showing that the range of spelling ability becomes greater as students progress through school. A typical third-grade class has students spelling from the first-grade to fourth-grade levels, while a typical group of sixth-graders has students ranging in ability from just below fourth grade to the high-school levels. The research points to the importance of selecting and using spelling materials in an ungraded and self-paced manner. It is as unfair to expect all fourth-graders to use a single fourth-grade textbook as it would be to expect them all to wear size 14 shoes that only a few could find comfortable. Students working below their academic level are just as unmotivated as students working with programs far above their level.

The major reason for the differences in spelling progress is that students differ widely in learning style. The effectiveness of spelling instruction seems to be more affected by the student's learning style than instruction in any other subject. Spelling is usually taught in a highly visual way. Students with weak visualization skills suffer the most through traditional approaches. Hildreth suggested that multisensory methods would level the playing field. G. A. Vergason further found that even students who are primarily visual learners also profit from multisensory methods, because such methods leave a stronger neural impression of the words. The stronger the impressions are, the easier students recall the information. Multisensory methods prove to be the most efficient for all learner styles.

In addition to placing individual students at the point in spelling programs most suitable to their achievement level, the pace at which students are expected to master the words must be individually determined. Assigning a weekly word list has definite disadvantages if each student must master the whole list. In traditional approaches, too often the words are assigned on Monday, tested on Friday, and forgotten on Saturday. Through research on how memory functions, we now know that the first teaching of a word is only the introduction to the learning process, which should include a long sequence of systematic presentations and reviews.

The primary way that pace can be adjusted in spelling instruction is through add-a-word lists. C. A. McGuigan introduced this concept in 1975. In this method, a group of words is pretested, and the misspelled words are studied. Words are retested until the student spells them correctly at least once. New words are added as old words are mastered. Students learn words more quickly using add-a-word lists and retain the correct spelling better than students using fixed-word lists.

The method by which students are tested can also have significant effect on their ability to learn words. Thomas Horn found in 1947 that simply correcting each word as it was tested provided tremendous gains in spelling achievement. Horn termed the procedure *immediate self-correction*. This step is important in English because there are so many possible spellings for so many sounds. Students easily become puzzled about the correct choice for the word being tested or written. Immediate self-correction gives them feedback before they forget what aspect of the word caused the problem. Thus students learn from their mistakes.

Effective spelling instruction is not limited to methods used to learn and test words. We must provide more than lists of words to memorize if we want to ensure that our students are able to spell the words they need to write now and in the future. We must also teach phonetic principles, spelling rules, and the use of spelling resources such as the dictionary.

No spelling program can teach all of the approximately six hundred thousand English words. An effective spelling program should teach at least the five thousand or so most frequently used words in such a way that students learn how to continue adding words to their vocabulary throughout their lives. A primary way to meet this goal is to integrate spelling instruction with the entire school program. Spelling cannot be taught in a vacuum but must become an active, integral part of each subject.

Ideas in Language Arts
Rachel Mackson

I share here a few ideas to get you started in language arts education. Although these tidbits are not a complete program, they do provide a starting point to help you on your way.

Reading

For our family, a combination of phonics and sight-reading has worked well. The study of phonics has provided a good foundation, as well as the skills necessary to decode new words. The English language, however, contains words that do not fit the phonetic system. In addition, once children pass the early decoding stage, they often read words as a whole. For these reasons, I use both methods to teach reading. Within a general framework combining phonics and sight-reading, each of my children has learned to read in a different manner.

Initially, sight-reading made no sense to my son. He liked the logic of phonics and enjoyed controlled vocabulary phonics readers. Once he was reading confidently in these books, he moved on to harder material but still preferred editions with a limited number of words. After slowly and surely building his reading ability, he moved beyond these books and now reads from a wide variety of selections.

My daughter, on the other hand, learns many words by their spelling and by how they look. She constantly asks,

"Mom, how do you spell such and such?" She readily figures out how to read irregular sight words and is not put off in the least by difficult books. One of her favorite activities is snuggling up on the sofa with a parent as she happily picks out any words she can read. Nonetheless, learning phonics has helped her. She is able to approach new words by sounding them out, something she could not do reading by sight alone.

Both of my school-age children have been helped in obtaining a phonics foundation by the *Sound Beginnings* program, which is available from Our Father's House. Because my children do not need all the repetition provided, I do not use all the dictation exercises. We also enhance our studies with flashcards and homemade games. When my son was reluctant to practice his phonics, I got a bag of mini-chocolate chips and let him have one for each phonogram he read correctly. I am not sure that bribery is the best way to teach, but at times it can be useful to get a child over a rough spot.

I recently discovered the *Little Angel Readers: Catholic Phonics Series*, produced by a Catholic homeschooling family, and the delightful stories in these readers are ideal for my daughter. She is also enjoying Seton's new full-color workbooks, *Kindergarten Phonics for Young Catholics*.

Writing

My approach to writing is eclectic. Over the years we have kept journals, done copy work, and used several other methods. All are effective, but we alternate, because overuse of any one technique tends to get dull.

For a reluctant writer like my son, it is somewhat overwhelming to produce original material as well as to remember spelling, punctuation, and capitalization, so I break these tasks apart. Sometimes he will dictate a story as I type at the computer or write in a notebook. Other times, he will copy a selected passage from a book, an excellent way to work on spelling and punctuation. I combine subjects by having my son copy from religion or history books. I also ask him to write in a journal, although not on a daily or even weekly basis. In the journal, I allow free rein and do not correct errors.

The best way to learn to write is just to do it. I explain that writing is like talking or thinking. If you can say it or think it, you can write it. In this area, my younger children have benefitted. Paper and pencils are kept handy, and places are set up for them to write. I was helped by the ideas presented in the Institute for Excellence in Writing workshop.

I suggest letting the children see you write. Getting published is better. Children are excited to see your writing in print. Another option is to write letters to relatives. Children who see you write to their grandparents are likely to do the same.

Mechanics of Writing

I have yet to find an ideal program for the mechanics of writing. There are many programs, and each has its own strengths and weaknesses.

The 1962 editions of *Voyages in English*, available from Kolbe Academy, are useful grammar texts for children in third grade through eighth grade. They require more time from Mom than workbook programs but promote thoughtfulness on the child's part. We have also enjoyed *Mad Libs*, which offer grammar with humor. *Mad Libs* are available at any bookstore. Our latest discovery has been the *Grammar Rock* computer program. It is definitely "edutainment", but my son has learned much as he plays.

Seton is publishing an *English for Young Catholics* series, similar in content to the *Voyages in English* series for grades one and two. You can count on a strong emphasis on mechanics, composition, and solidly Catholic content. This series is currently available for first, second, and sixth grade.

Handwriting

I experimented with the italic method and found it useful. Some will find it easier for their children to read and write standard print and cursive. Seton produces a basic series, *Handwriting for Young Catholics*.

Vocabulary

I strongly believe that children increase their vocabulary by reading and being read to, but I also feel that as children get older the *Wordly Wise* vocabulary series, available through Seton, is valuable, but not strictly necessary.

I hope that these suggestions help you get started and give you a feel for how language arts can progress in the homeschool.

Language is the expression of ideas, and if the people of one country cannot preserve an identity of ideas they cannot retain an identity of language.

— Noah Webster, Preface to Dictionary, 1828 ed.

Drew's Reading Journey
Cindy Garrison

Reading has been an interesting experience in our homeschool. Our daughter began reading when she was four. She caught on quickly to sounding out words and liked reading stories. By age seven or eight, she was reading fluently and comprehended well. Now, at age ten, she works independently on most of her schoolwork and enjoys leisure reading.

Our son, who is now eight, was entirely different. I attempted to introduce him to reading at age five, with no success. He was not interested, and I had read that boys develop slower than girls, so I did not push it. At age six, we tried again. He would read the primers and did well at learning to sound out words. I noticed that he would add other words to the sentences he was reading, but since these were kindergarten primers, I was not too concerned. The next year, his reading progressed slowly. He read the readers, but not very quickly. He still added words to his sentences and he could not comprehend what he read. He began to get frustrated. I was beginning to think he might have a learning disability. He also had problems writing answers on the correct lines, but when he answered verbally, he could get them all right.

We decided to have his eyes checked at the end of first grade because there had not been much reading progress through that year. His eyes jumped all over, and he picked up words from other sentences. He was not comprehending what he read because it did not make sense. His vision was fine, but he failed every test that checked his visual tracking.

Once we knew the problem, we began a whole new approach to his schooling. First we prayed together as a family for his vision to improve. Sometimes, I would make the sign of the cross on his eyelids. Then we began doing all his second-grade school work orally. He did eye exercises, dot-to-dots, mazes, and word searches to help his tracking ability. We went back to reading slowly, and he read using a bookmark under each sentence. He began to realize when a word did not belong in a sentence and started comprehending what he read. He had a whole new attitude and began feeling confident again. We believe God helped him improve.

About six months ago, he became interested in sports scores, so I had him reading the local sports page. I also made available lots of books on insects and animals, since he is interested in those topics. Using books where his interests lie has helped him and keeps him interested in reading.

He has just begun the third grade and is reading better. We do not do as much of his work verbally as we used to. While he is reading he can realize when things do not make sense, and then he will reread the sentence. He still needs a bookmark and is a little slower reading aloud than some children his age, but he is making progress.

I feel that because I worked one-on-one with my son, his vision problem was discovered as soon as possible. Had his tracking difficulty been ignored until upper-elementary age, it may have been too late. We truly believe that homeschooling has been a blessing in this situation. Once the problem was diagnosed, we were immediately able to individualize his schoolwork. This will be an ongoing process, but our ability to adjust our curriculum to fit the needs of our son is exactly what he needed. He was not labeled, teased, or made to feel different. His self-esteem remained intact, and his self-confidence came back quickly. We are looking forward to continued progress in his future.

O give thanks to the Lord, for he is good; his steadfast love endures for ever!

—Psalm 118:1

History Unfolding

Rachel Mackson

I wanted my children to get a good view of history in sequence, so I began by reading a children's Bible history to my son in the first grade. In the second grade, I used an easy children's Bible as my son's reader. I felt this laid a good foundation in Old Testament history.

About halfway through the second-grade year, I heard about Greenleaf's history units, which can be purchased from Emmanuel Books. Although Greenleaf is not a Catholic company, its material on ancient history is excellent. I sent away for the Egypt package. We learned a great deal, and history became one of our favorite topics. For the most part, we read the books and did only some of the recommended activities. One of the projects that attracted us, however, was building a pyramid with sugar cubes. When I did not have any on hand, my husband suggested using Lego bricks. Building pyramids engaged my son's interest for many days.

We continued in the third grade with the Greenleaf program, this time choosing ancient Greece, since it was next chronologically. We particularly liked *The Greeks* from Ursborne Books, *The Children's Homer*, and *Famous Men of Greece*. When we finished these books, I happened to start reading aloud *Tales from Shakespeare*, a collection of Shakespeare's plays rewritten for children by Charles and Mary Lamb. We quickly noticed that many of these were about Greeks and picked out those particular plays to read. Coincidentally, we were also reading *Number Stories of Long*

Ago, which fit in well. Since many of the first mathematicians were Greeks, we made further connections by reading select biographies from *Mathematicians Are People Too*.

After such an immersion, my son expressed a desire to learn Greek. *English from the Roots Up*, available from Emmanuel Books, has many Greek words and provided a simple beginning. My son, however, wanted to learn the language, so I ordered the only Greek resource that I could find, *New Testament Greek in 30 Minutes a Day*, which I located in the Kolbe Academy catalog. The interest in all things Greek continued, and we found an old movie on Alexander the Great at the video store.

The movie sparked an interest in what really happened. We looked up Alexander in *Christ the King, Lord of History*, published by TAN Books, and found that the movie had been historically accurate. An added benefit of seeing the movie was that my son was able to visualize the Greek innovations in war tactics. Army formations were important to Alexander's victories, and I doubt that my son would have understood the advantage gained by the unique shapes formed by the soldiers and their shields without seeing them in action.

I am fortunate to live in the center of Michigan where there have been several homeschool conferences and book fairs at which I can browse. At one conference, I found and purchased *A Histomap of World History*, from Rand McNally. The *Histomap* is a vertical timeline showing the ebb and flow of civilizations. I laminated it and hung it in a visible location leading down the hall. This timeline has sparked many questions. My children will stop and try to figure it out. Not only that, but my son became interested and made his own chart showing the development of weapons throughout ancient and modern history. He also guessed what people looked like before the Egyptians and drew their pictures. There was a huge break in his timeline between the ancient and the modern world, but my son did know that there was a gap, knowledge that I see as a real plus. When we eventually get to the Middle Ages, he will already know where they belong in history.

After our positive experience with the *Histomap*, I heard about the reprinting of *Old World and America*, by TAN books, and purchased it. *Old World* has been outstanding for reading aloud and has added a solid Catholic dimension to our studies. Furthermore, the book correlates almost perfectly with the *Histomap*.

Based on my good experience with *Old World*, I ordered *Our Pioneers and Patriots*, by the same author. I had planned to use it for the next year, fourth grade, but just as the book arrived, my son became interested in U.S. history while playing the computer game *America Rocks*. He wanted to begin immediately, so I started reading the book aloud. *Pioneers* gives a good overview with just the right amount of information for introductory studies. Moreover, I already had part of the *Childhood of Famous Americans* series, and my son began reading some of these titles.

The interest in the United States is almost as strong as is the interest in Greece, and history remains one of our favorite subjects. We plan to finish our investigation of U.S. history and then to study the Romans. Chronologically, they came right after the Greeks and incorporate much of the Grecian culture. Studying them next will help my children understand the flow of Western civilization.

Because future plans include Latin, I am considering purchasing *Our Roman Roots*, by Dr. Leek. It combines the study of Roman history, Church history, and Latin. I have also obtained a reprint of *Augustus Caesar's World*. This book covers the history of Rome at the time immediately before and after the birth of Christ. We can use it for reading aloud, along with the matching sections from *Old World*. I am also budgeting for the *History through the Saints* timeline, produced by Catholic Heritage Curricula. I hope it will spark a similar burst of interest in Church history.

Another option we are contemplating is *The Parables of Christ*, reprinted by Roman Catholic Books. Included in the text is a copy of each parable in English, Greek, and Latin. Comparing translations is like decoding secret messages. Studying Scripture in these three languages should be an exciting tie-in to our Greek, Roman, and religion studies. My son is looking forward to this prospect. One of his favorite parts of *New Testament Greek in 30 Minutes a Day* was looking up the Bible passages in English in order to translate the Scripture passages sprinkled in the lessons.

At this point, I have switched to using *The Old World and America* as the backbone of my history studies. I plan to follow this text through the course of history, supplementing with good reading materials, biographies of the saints, and movies. These sources provide links between religious studies, language studies, and the *Histomap*. Furthermore, I will read related sections of *Christ the King, Lord of History* myself, so that I have a good picture of each time period and can answer the children's questions knowledgeably. This kind of support is one of the best ways to draw out my children's ability to make connections themselves. We remain free to pursue interests in specific historical periods as they arise and find *The Kingfisher Illustrated History of the World* an excellent, although secular, book for the children to browse.

This report may sound as though I pulled it together deliberately, but in reality, the connections came about in a rather haphazard manner. We did not make daily, or even weekly, connections between the various resources. Rather, these occurred at various intervals, some a month, if not longer, apart. Most importantly, it was not Mom who made all the connections. Many came about because of a child's interest in a topic or by a child asking probing questions during read-aloud time.

I share these experiences in the hope that beginning homeschool mothers will not feel intimidated by thinking they must start with a detailed plan in order to have successful history studies. We certainly did not. As the years progressed, we just stumbled upon things. Keep in mind though, that we stumbled upon things because there was such an abundance of available resources and because we were always on the lookout.

If, by chance, you do not feel up to the task of guiding your child through the centuries of history, Julia Fogassy of Our Father's House has produced a marvelous, but expensive, program: *The ABCs of Christian Culture.*

The Histomap may be purchased from Rand McNally at (800) 777-8132.

The life that is unexamined is not worth living.

—Plato

Science Studies
Rachel Mackson

My experience has led me to believe that it is not necessary to do a great deal of formal science in early elementary education. The time to study in depth begins in junior and senior high. For younger children, the libraries are now full of colorful, fact-filled science books. Sparking a child's interest with titles such as the *Science Encyclopedia* published by Dorling Kindersley or anything from *The Magic School Bus* series takes almost no effort from the parents. The authors have gone to great length to make science approachable and at the same time have provided abundant information.

On television, there are free programs such as *Bill Nye, The Science Guy*; *The Magic School Bus*; and so many more that it is impossible to list them. My kids love these shows, but I do not let them watch on a daily basis. I purchased the video set *The Wonders of God's Creation* from the Ignatius Press catalog. These tapes add a much-needed godly perspective to our science studies, since most TV shows are decidedly secular.

I begin our homeschooling science with sporadic nature studies. Nature study starts when I share my awe over the wonders of God's world with my children. I marvel at beautiful flowers, sunsets, and whatever insects happen to cross our path. I give each child a notebook of unlined paper and occasionally ask for a sketch of a plant or insect. To sketch, a child must pay attention to detail, thus providing practice in close observation, an important scientific skill. *The Usborne Complete First Book of Nature* is appealing to children and filled with information.

Through the years, I have sought a decent textbook, convinced I needed one. In my opinion, most science texts for early elementary children are shallow. They attempt to cover a huge range of topics but cannot do so in depth. Eventually, I ended up going to the bookstore with my son to purchase books of his choice on science with the money budgeted for a textbook. There was so much to choose from that he took a long time to decide. He ended up with three glossy and surprisingly informative books. I have since discovered the sale table at Barnes and Noble Booksellers, which we scan for inexpensive science books every time we visit.

At a homeschool conference, I saw a set of cartoon books by Larry Gonick and Art Huffman. When I first saw them, I thought, "No way can a kid learn science from a book of cartoons." My son has proven me wrong. The volume on physics is particularly good.

I still feel guilty for not matching the exciting hands-on experiments done at our local schools and assuage my guilt by taking the kids to children's museums and an occasional science demonstration. We usually go once a year, which seems to be enough. It is all right to wait for a child to learn to enjoy these activities independently. Children do not need a big show put on by an adult. They can work individually and have fun at home dismantling old toasters, VCRs, and other broken appliances in an attempt to understand how they work.

Some of the most important scientific discoveries were made by people curious to learn how the world works. In your own home, you can provide opportunities for children to mess around and make independent discoveries.

Do not underestimate the power of a good book to stimulate interest and learning. Just as in teaching math, the teaching of science is enhanced by reading biographies of scientists and by studying topics of interest. It is difficult to encourage an unfamiliar subject, but if a parent needs a refresher, *Science Matters: Achieving Scientific Literacy*, by Robert M. Hazen and James Trefil, offers a concise overview.

Microscopes can be fun, as can computer CD-ROMs that provide realistic simulation. A child can often see more on a computer program than would be possible with an inexpensive microscope. Keep in mind, however, that you can get along fine without either the microscope or the computer program. The most important skill for a scientist is the ability to observe closely. This skill can be practiced easily on objects large enough to be seen without magnification.

Nothing interests children quite like simple science experiments, and there are many books currently available. Most include a wide range of activities, but be wary. I find the majority to be overkill, so let me end by describing three extremely easy hands-on science activities. Most use common household ingredients. I leave to your imagination the talk by which you introduce the experiments.

1. To demonstrate a chemical reaction that cleans.
You need a handful of tarnished pennies, a cup or so of vinegar, salt, and a small, clear container with a lid.

Put the pennies in the container, fill about halfway with vinegar, and pour in several tablespoons of salt. Put on the lid and shake. Let the children check the progress. Soon, the old pennies will be shiny and bright. Wow!

2. To demonstrate a chemical reaction that expands.
You need vinegar, baking soda, and some kind of clay. If you do not have clay handy, any old container will do.

When vinegar and baking soda are mixed, they fizz and make a mess; therefore have the children do this one outdoors. They use the clay to make a volcano with a crater at the top. The vinegar-and-baking-soda mix in the crater causes a "lava flow". My kids also have fun filling an old margarine tub, shaking it, and watching (from a safe distance) for the lid to pop off. Usually the tub fizzes over, but the occasional popped lid keeps them repeating this for hours.

3. To demonstrate expansion during a changing state.
You need a balloon and dry ice.

Using gloves, put a small piece of dry ice inside the balloon and tie it tightly shut. Then watch as the balloon slowly expands. This display demonstrates expansion of a chemical compound as it changes states.

Finding dry ice is not too difficult. You might try calling a friendly teacher or school. Ice-cream parlors and convenience stores will sometimes sell dry ice. This experiment is worth the trouble!

Science is a first-rate piece of furniture for a man's upper chamber, if he has common sense on the ground floor.

—Oliver Wendell Holmes, *The Poet at the Breakfast Table*

Chapter 4

Ideas for Enrichment

Nothing sublimely artistic has ever arisen out of mere art, any more than anything essentially reasonable has ever arisen out of pure reason. There must always be a rich moral soil for any great aesthetic growth.

—G. K. Chesterton

Playing in the Dirt
Maureen Wittmann

One day last spring, my children asked for their own garden. They love helping me weed, prune, and water the plants. Now they wanted their own seedlings to care for. We began with a trip to the local nursery. I let them choose the vegetables and flowers themselves. After much debate between my four- and six-year-olds, carrots, cherry tomatoes, sweet peppers, onions, and impatiens were decided upon.

After arriving home, they had to decide on a plot. Following a long discussion on the importance of sunlight and good drainage, they found the perfect spot just under the kitchen window. They all agreed that it was best to grow food close to the place you eat. They marked off their plot and were ready to plant.

At least they thought they were ready. Mom had to intervene and tell them about the importance of aeration and nutrients in the soil. Off to the shed they went to gather shovels and rakes, and they began to till. I must tell you, there is nothing funnier than a two-year-old trying to dig with a full-size shovel. This was an all-day project. By the end of the day, they were covered with dirt and totally wiped out. The yard was a sight as well.

They were bright-eyed and bushy-tailed early the next morning, ready to get back to work. Unfortunately, I was not. It was tempting to send them off to the swing set until I downed another cup of coffee, but I did not want to squash their enthusiasm. So off we went, at 8:00 in the morning, to play in the dirt. The children pointed out that they had aerated the soil the day before; now it was time feed the soil. A discussion of how nutrients get into the soil ensued. We talked about the beauty of God's design in nature, how everything from the apple core to the fallen leaf turns back into the earth and then turns around and feeds new vegetation. Suddenly, the lightbulbs began to go on. Fallen leaves, nutrients, fallen leaves, nutrients, fallen leaves—ah, there was a massive mound of leaves in the woods behind our play yard.

Every year we rake our leaves into the woods rather than overburden the local landfill with thirty bags of yard waste. We circled the leaf mountain and eyed it up and down. It looked like a simple pile of leaves, but what was waiting for us underneath? Off they went to the shed again. They grabbed everything in sight, including gloves, shovels, rakes, trowels, and our trusty red Radio Flyer wagon. They flew down to the woods, tools and wagon in tow. We all began to dig. The deeper we dug into the pile, the more decomposed the leaves became. Toward the bottom we found zillions of earthworms—well, not quite zillions. The children found it fascinating that the worms eat the decomposing leaves and then return them back to the earth providing better soil for new plant growth. The lightbulbs were going on all over the place now!

After filling the Radio Flyer with rich, sweet-smelling compost, we prepared our garden for planting. I showed them how to measure the distance between seedlings, so that their plants had room to prosper. One by one, they dug holes, carefully measuring the depth and planting their future harvest. I was covered from head to toe with dirt; I was sweaty and itchy, yet I had never felt better in my life.

That was only the beginning. The summer was spent weeding, pruning, and watering. The great part was they did most of it on their own. Once the garden was in place, I did not help with its maintenance. I did have to remind them from time to time to water, but they took full responsibility of their charge. Of course, when you take responsibility, you get to reap the benefits. They enjoyed picnics in the backyard with carrots and cherry tomatoes sweet as sugar, all while admiring their flowers.

What did the children learn from the garden project? They learned about photosynthesis, composting, responsibility, God's creation, organic gardening, math, and more. Whether you have your hands in the dirt or your nose in a book, homeschooling is about learning all the time. And the best part is the children are not the only ones receiving an education. Sometimes Mom picks up a piece of knowledge here and there.

What did Mom learn? I already knew about photosynthesis and the rest, but I think I learned a more important lesson. Just a short time ago, my life was about my career, driving a nice car, and belonging to the right club. Now my life is about playing in the dirt with my children. I am so glad that I finally grew up.

Truly, I say to you, whoever does not receive the kingdom of God like a child shall not enter it. And then he took them in his arms and blessed them, laying his hands upon them.

—Mark 10:15–16

Latin: Getting Our Toes Wet
Becky Wissner

I encourage anyone beginning homeschooling to seek out a homeschool group. Involvement with our group has been delightfully enriching. And I do not think the need for an established prayer time can be overstated when one considers homeschooling and its demands. I found my relationship with God so necessary for a happy and holy family life and successful school experience that I wonder how I ever survived without prayer.

Our homeschool has benefitted greatly from tips and good practices we have learned from other homeschool families. One such practice is the teaching of Latin. Since many of my friends were teaching the subject, I decided to give Latin a try, despite the fact that I had never studied it myself. I purchased the *Latina Christiana* program, from Catholic Heritage Curricula. It has proven to be an effective course for my fourth-grade child. It comes with a weekly lesson plan that includes ancient Roman history and geography studies along with word etymology and the memorization of Latin itself, including prayers and songs. It includes a pronunciation tape, a teacher book, and a student book.

One unexpected and important thing I learned when I began was to read over my materials more thoroughly. I was giving my child one lesson a day instead of one lesson a week. As a result, the program was going entirely too fast, and my child and I were stressed. In frustration, I finally read the teacher's book and realized my mistake.

The program is great, but I have not been implementing the full lesson. We leave out much of the history and geography and concentrate on the vocabulary and etymology. My daughter does her flashcards, memorizes the prayers, and writes the words. She thinks the etymology is fun! There is no rule that says she has to know Latin at a certain age, so I take the program at a pace she can handle comfortably.

I utilize the text as a base of information and pick and choose what we feel is of benefit to our family. I may use the same book next year, reviewing the vocabulary and picking up the history and geography, so that we can do a more in-depth study. The second round will provide an excellent review as well as enrichment. I do hope that by the end of high school, my children will have a good command of Latin. But why rush? Reading and math are essential; Latin is an enriching extra.

Although I consider Latin an extra, it is an important part of our curriculum. Much of our Catholic heritage and our own American government are based on the language of the Roman empire. Many of the great literary works of our Catholic culture are best understood in their original language. Studying Latin has helped expand our family's understanding of our country and the Church. At this time, no child in the family can read a book written in Latin. Perhaps none will ever get to that point. But for now, we enjoy getting our toes wet. Without our homeschooling friends, we might never have been brave enough even to get near the water.

Geography on the Go
Rachel Mackson

The most important step when determining your course of study in geography is to set goals. The topic is so broad. There are many styles of teaching, so thinking beforehand will help. Kolbe Academy sells a nice set of workbooks called *Map Skills*. These workbooks provide one effective approach to the subject, and we have enjoyed using them on occasion.

I considered the basics—reading, 'riting, 'rithmetic, and religion—to be the most important topics, and I added in subjects like geography only as I felt more confident. My goals were for my children to be familiar with globes and maps and to have a good idea where most countries are located. Eventually, I would like them to know where all the states are, although I have not set memorization as an aim for our family.

With these rather general goals in mind, I made sure to have a globe always handy and often stopped to look up places that we read about in our books. Reference to a globe is one of the handiest ways to become familiar with the location of the countries around the world. Hearing about a place provides a spark of interest to get a child involved. Once their curiosity is whetted, the children ask many questions about all those funny lines on the globe, which in turn prompts many more conversations. I answer the children's questions to the best of my ability. If I do not know an answer, we look it up together.

I have found that a good map, posted at the children's eye level, draws out many questions. On the spur of the moment, we found the city where Grandma lives and picked out the places where we have vacationed. In addition, even if you never leave your home state, children can easily learn geography by locating nearby cities on a state map. It can also be fun to plan fantasy trips using an atlas or globe. Pick a spot, then try to determine the best route to get there. None of these activities need to be done frequently to be successful.

Since one of my goals was to have my children familiar with the United States, I purchased a *Laurie* foam map of the U.S. and a *Wee Sing America* tape. They were our second-grade geography program. The *Carmen Sandiego* CD-ROM enhanced our geography studies in the third grade. For next year, fourth grade, I plan to purchase tapes singing the states and their capitals. Listening to tapes in the car has proven to work well. I have also purchased *The DK Geography of the World* from Dorling Kindersley. It is an excellent book for independent browsing by children and includes simple maps, sketches, and many photos.

If you have read any of my other essays, you know that I cannot end without mentioning at least one literature resource. The books by Holling C. Holling (*Minn of Mississippi*, *Paddle to the Sea*, etc.) are a great way to introduce U.S. geography. These titles are prime examples of how exciting the literature approach can be. They combine an entrancing story with geography and natural science. Of all our literature resources, my husband likes these best. They are available in a set with maps and unit study guide, but I think that the books can stand alone. Moreover, you can use whatever map you already have and save yourself any extra expense.

Geography is a subject you can make as little or as much of as you like. I prefer to concentrate on the basics and add in small amounts of geography as I find the time. A few activities scattered here and there among your studies can meet most geography goals.

The earth is the LORD's
  and the fulness thereof,
the world and those who dwell therein.

—Psalm 24:1

Learning to Love Music
Karen Urness

Stepping into our home at any given time, you may find your senses awakened. Our house is noisy. Not the noise of screaming and discontentment, but the noise of musical instruments being played. It is not uncommon to hear an accordion, piano, cello, clarinet, violin, or flute—and many times a combination of four of these at once. We have a small home, and for some reason the children all enjoy practicing at the same time. Each of our four school-aged children seizes a different corner of the house in which to rehearse.

Since my husband and I were music majors in college, we told our children it was required to learn an instrument in order to stay in the family. Of course, we were teasing them, but, wishing to encourage their music appreciation, we made every effort to surround our children with music and musical activities. For example, we take them to many different types of concerts. Our children have enjoyed symphony orchestras, jazz ensembles, small polka combos, and various ethnic groups. Taking the children to musical events accomplishes more than teaching a love for music. The children learn about music as an occupation, they learn how to behave in a more formal atmosphere, and most important, they build up a knowledge of instruments and composers.

Another method for encouraging music appreciation is to have many types of music available for the children's listening pleasure. It is helpful to collect recordings of the famous composers from different eras: baroque, romantic, classical, modern, and others. Finding a nice selection of jazz and contemporary music will also enhance their understanding and love of music. Pieces written just for children, such as *Peter and the Wolf*, are also a good idea. The *Classical Kids* series combines the music of great composers along with their biographies in a fun format. We often play this music in our home, as background, while the children are busy with their schoolwork.

In addition to providing audio recordings of music, it is also helpful to have books on many different composers available for the children. A short trip to the library can offer biographies on Beethoven, Bach, Liszt, as well as many contemporary artists. Reading about these wonderful composers gives added depth and understanding of them and their compositions.

Besides saturating the children's atmosphere with music, I recommend having good quality instruments available for the children to practice. Do not rush out and pick up any yard-sale offering that you can find. Many of these are in poor condition. It is challenging enough to learn a new instrument without fighting with cracks, leaks, dents, and overall poor workmanship. If you locate an instrument through a newspaper advertisement, make certain that you bring along someone knowledgeable. Renting is an excellent way to become familiar with an instrument without a serious financial commitment. (Most music stores offer a rental program.) If the child finds that his tuba is not what he hoped for, you are not out thousands of dollars.

I advise a child to sign up for private music lessons before bringing his violin or flute home. It is difficult to learn an instrument well without instruction. After your child takes lessons for a while, you may wish to go one step farther and enroll him in some sort of large ensemble. Playing music is more enjoyable when you can share it with a group.

We are able to have our children participate in the local public school's band and orchestra program. Our children have made new friends, learned how an ensemble performs together, and have appreciated their instruments more than ever. If this option is not available to you, try calling your nearby symphony orchestra to find out whether they have a children's group available. Most likely, an audition will be required, but after taking private lessons, your child will be ready for the challenge. Last of all, it is important not to put the instrument on a high shelf or in a closet but to keep it out so the child will see it and be reminded to practice.

Music is such an integral part of our lives. I feel it is ingrained in the people that we are. It is difficult to imagine our home without the squeaks, clinks, and beautiful melodies our children are learning to play. If you were to ask, they would tell you that music is their favorite subject. It is mine too!

Musical training is a more potent instrument than any other, because rhythm and harmony find their way into the inward places of the soul.

—Plato, *The Republic*

Teaching Art When You Are Not Artistic
Cindy Garrison, Maureen Wittmann, and Rachel Mackson

Cindy's Turn . . .

I am not particularly artistic, but crafts I can do. My children have made angels out of crochet yarn and crosses out of ribbon, decorated grapevine wreaths, and arranged pressed flowers, but I can barely draw a stick person! Drawing, painting, blending, working with colors, and molding clay are things I have no talent for. Fortunately, where I have weaknesses in art, my husband has strengths. He can draw and shade so that everything looks lifelike.

We decided to pool our strengths and tackle art together. I work on craft projects, and my husband teaches the children drawing and related subjects. We do not have a set schedule but do projects as they come up. To record their progress and to give them something special to keep, we make a portfolio of each child's drawings. Spending time with Dad in the evenings, working on art, has become one of our children's favorite pastimes. They have used *Art with a Purpose* packs, which we bought from Catholic Heritage Curricula, and the book *What Shall I Draw?* as a supplement.

Working together as a team has been a great experience to share with our children. It also makes Dad feel less like an outsider and more like the valuable asset he is to our homeschool.

Maureen's Turn . . .

I often find art products at garage sales and libraries. One treasure was a book titled *Please Touch*. The author suggests that giving children a blank sheet of paper will encourage more creativity than giving them a coloring book page or an assigned project.

How do I approach art? I give my children free access to crayons, markers, paints, stickers, scrap paper, tape, holy cards, stamps, hole punchers, scissors, homemade play dough, glue, yarn, string, old buttons, glitter, rulers, and stencils. I find many of these goodies at garage sales. The result has been an astounding success. The children come up with all kinds of wonderful originals, including avant-garde sculptures, comic books, three-dimensional paint-ings, beautiful religious pieces, self-portraits, and so on. Creativity is flowing freely at our house.

My son has expressed an interest in learning more about technique, so I supply him with how-to books from the library. Where my talents fail, he is educating himself through experimentation and through books. I believe what he is learning in art will stay with him, because he is driven more by his own desire than by mine.

Occasionally, I organize art projects for the children. Our favorite, making rosaries, did not begin as an art project, but as one of charity. The children and I started a rosary-making guild in our homeschool support group. We donate our homemade rosaries to the missions, where they are desperately needed. This small act of charity has turned into a regular unit study in religion, math, and art.

We pray, count beads, and play around with the possible color combinations.

What is my advice to fellow homeschoolers short on talent? Give your little ones blank white paper and a few supplies, and you will not believe the creations that find their way to your refrigerator door.

Rachel's Turn . . .

Art Appreciation

I used to think of art appreciation as an intimidating subject, but I no longer do. At first, I chose complicated and expensive resources like *Mommy, It's a Renoir!*, which can be purchased from Emmanuel Books. We had great fun with this program, although it is expensive. I do not regret the purchase, but lately we have been taking a simpler approach.

Charlotte Mason's idea of having a child describe great paintings appeals to me. This practice helps a child develop attention to detail and is easy to implement. All it involves is showing a picture to the child for one to five minutes, putting the picture face down, and then asking the child to describe what he can remember. It is important not to expect too much on the first try. Over time, you will definitely see improvement.

When a child is good at describing, you can move on to the next step: having the child sketch the picture from memory. Use the same procedure, but instead of requesting a description with words, ask for a drawing. If a child is reluctant, gently encourage him to do the best he can and describe the painting with a picture. The reproduction will look childish, of course, but that is fine. The important part is remembering the detail; artistic talent is secondary.

You do not have to be a master artist to appreciate a good painting.

Finding good art is not a problem if you own any of the titles in the *Faith and Life* catechism series published by Ignatius Press. Every chapter, with the exception of the second-grade volume, begins with a beautiful work of religious art. Both the name of the painting and the name of the artist are listed in the back of the book. Finding the time for this subject is simple: add it to the religion unit. Combining studies makes art appreciation easy and accessible.

I occasionally purchase an inexpensive poster of a good painting and hang it in a visible location in the children's playroom. By periodically changing the picture, I can expose them to a number of paintings in the course of several years. I also buy quality art reproductions, nicely framed, to decorate the house. The art on the walls of the home will, over time, influence the children's taste. Sophia Institute Press and the Leaflet Missal Company are both good sources of beautiful religious art. Ignatius Press offers lovely art videos, and I hope that our budget will allow us to purchase a set highlighting Vatican art.

A more formal study of art appreciation would be wonderful. Maybe in time, we will work up to that. For now, however, we are content to keep a relaxed routine.

Drawing
My children love to draw. They want to learn how to create realistic pictures, so I have on hand various *How to Draw* books for each child's specific interests. These titles can be found in many libraries. Bruce McIntyre's *Drawing Textbook* is inexpensive and helpful if you do not know how to make pictures look three-dimensional.

I also provide lots of tracing paper. I was initially afraid that tracing would inhibit creativity, but it has not. As a matter of fact, it has helped my children's drawing ability and handwriting because the fine motor skills involved in drawing, tracing, and writing are so similar. Recently, my son has enjoyed *Lamb's Book of Art*. The book begins with the study of primary and secondary hues and continues with complementary colors and various drawing techniques. Lessons are specific, but Mr. Lamb encourages creative expression throughout.

Degrade first the arts if you'd mankind degrade.

—William Blake

How Much Is That Doggie in the Window?

Dani Foster Herring

My eldest son, Sean, wanted a puppy for Christmas. "Fine," said I, "but you're going to have to do a lot of research. You have to see what type of dog would fit into our family and how much time, effort, and money will be involved."

"Where do I begin?" he wailed. On the Internet.

We spend a lot of time together on the Internet perusing museums and art galleries, reading online stories, reading about experiments performed on Twinkies, downloading wav (sound) and bmp (picture) files for use in our desktop themes and graphic programs. We have even performed a virtual dissection on a cow's eye.

The Internet is full of wonderful places to visit, but it also offers practical information right at your fingertips. Using a search engine, Sean was able to find more information than one person could process in a lifetime on the different breeds of dogs. He quickly found websites with pictures and details about each breed's strengths and weaknesses. Upon finding an online test designed to match a dog to one's preferences and specifications (i.e., yard size, time spent grooming, ages of family members, etc.), he was able to narrow his choice.

A Brittany spaniel was decided upon, a medium-sized dog requiring little grooming, with high energy and a good temperament (needed with two-year-old twins). Then it was back to the computer to find a breeder. With the help of the American Kennel Club (AKC) website, we were able to locate a breeder in our area. Three days later, after a short trip to Virginia, Sean was the proud owner of Rusty Pupper, a large, beautiful, chestnut-and-white male with freckles on his nose.

Use of the Internet has continued, although it is no longer needed in the quest for the perfect dog. At the AKC website, my son found information on AKC's *Best Friend Program*, which he requested and quickly received. Rusty's breeder is active on the Brittany board on America On-line's Pet Care Forum. She and Sean have corresponded back and forth via e-mail on various dog-training issues. She directed him to a website that has a picture of Rusty's dad, FC Linvel's Blazin' Jake. Sean downloaded the picture and included it in a pet care booklet he made on the computer (an activity suggested by the "Best Friend" program). Dad took it to work to bind it, and we now have a nifty contribution to Sean's portfolio.

Sean has spent a lot of time, effort, and energy on this endeavor, and it has paid off handsomely: he has a dog that loves him, is good-natured with the little ones, and is a nice addition to our family. Not a bad accomplishment for a ten-year-old.

Educational Websites

The Super Site for Kids:
    http://www.bonus.com
Blue Web'n Home Page:
    http://www.kn.pacbell.com/wired/bluewebn

Dog Websites

AKC Homepage:
   http://www.akc.org/text/contents.htm
Pro Dog Networks:
   http://www.prodogs.com/indexf.htm
Pets 4 You:
   http://www.pets4you.com/home.html
CyberPet:
   http://www.cyberpet.com

All things bright and beautiful,
All creatures great and small,
All things wise and wonderful,
The Lord God made them all.

—Cecil Frances Alexander

Building Your Home Library
Maureen Wittmann

A home library is vital to your homeschool. Having a well-stocked, easily accessible home library opens up a world of information. Make your children feel comfortable going to the shelves and finding a good book to enjoy. Once your children start learning from books, the rest of home-schooling is much easier. For their sake, and yours, start building your home library.

The first step is to take inventory. You never know what you may find. Gather all your resource books, religious texts, and those old dusty classics. Rediscover all the treasures at home. Next, ask your parents for your childhood books. Sharing familiar stories with your children is a great experience. You may find that your children's favorites were also your favorites, and perhaps your parents' favorites as well.

You do not want to spend your entire household budget on books, so start inexpensively. Garage sales, library sales, and used-book stores are wonderful places to begin. I have found good classics in beautiful condition for as little as ten cents. Consider calling your local Catholic school or seminary. My husband rescued several boxes of old books from the trash bin at a diocesan seminary. One man's garbage is another man's treasure! Many bookstores extend their educators' discount to homeschoolers, so always ask for a discount before making a purchase.

Be choosy before you buy. Why buy mediocre books for your children, when great books are as easily available?

Quality does matter more than quantity. Do your home-work, ask other home educators, and read books such as *Honey for a Child's Heart* to guide your purchasing decisions. *Kolbe Academy Recommended Reading List* is another good resource. This can be purchased at a reasonable price or downloaded from their website.

Even if you now have a beautiful home library, the public library is still a good source for supplementing your stock. Check out books that you are considering for your home to make sure they are worth your hard-earned dollar. Also check out books that will be read only once. Last year, I read biographies of the great composers to my children. As we read about their lives, we also listened to their music. I could never have purchased a new biography and audio-cassette each week, but I could check them out of the library.

Do not assume that all books found in the children's section of the library are appropriate for reading by your young ones. Be sure to review all materials before taking them home (one reason to stick with those tried and true classics: you know the content is acceptable).

They say that kids are more likely to become avid readers if they see Mom and Dad reading. Do not forget a few books for yourself.

Books are the legacies that a great genius leaves to mankind, which are delivered down from generation to generation, as presents to the posterity of those who are yet unborn.

—Addison, *The Spectator*

Chapter 5

How We Homeschool

As it is the parents who have given life to their children, on them lies the gravest obligation of educating their family. They must therefore be recognized as being primarily and principally responsible for their education. The role of parents in education is of such importance that it is almost impossible to provide an adequate substitute. It is therefore the duty of parents to create a family atmosphere inspired by love and devotion to God and their fellow-men which will promote an integrated, personal and social education of their children

—Second Vatican Council,
Declaration on Christian Education

Homeschooling in the Large Family
Sue Kreiner

Homeschooling with a large family is a challenging, yet rewarding, experience. It has become a special way of life for us.

I strive to keep our home a haven of peace and tranquility. If the children are feeling rambunctious, they are sent outdoors or to the basement to play. No rowdy play or running is allowed in the house in order to preserve my peace of mind. We have numerous sacramentals on display in our home to remind us that Jesus is always present; therefore, we must behave as if he is a guest here.

We also limit outside activities. If each child were involved in even one or two different activities, we would have no home life at all. We try to choose activities that have a broad age range so that three or four children can participate in the same event. Of course, the children would prefer that they were involved in a lot more, but I would not be able to handle the stress over and above my responsibilities in the home. We get plenty of social interaction by doing service work within our parish and community. All parents have to consider prayerfully what works best for them and their family, without losing sight of the goals that God has for us.

When we do go away, each of the older children is responsible for a younger child. The older ones make sure their charges are dressed properly, with brushed hair and washed faces. The older children also help at meal times with serving the younger ones. I take responsibility for the baby. Although there is no set routine for helping each other with schoolwork, I often request that an older child quiz a younger one on math facts, religion, memory work, spelling, geography, or English. Repetition is necessary for the younger children. Besides the constant review and reinforcement that the older children get, this practice also teaches them patience, responsibility, and kindness. I hope that by instilling a cooperative and serving spirit within our family, I will see that spirit grow and extend toward our community as the children become adults.

Our typical day begins with breakfast and household chores. If our home is tidy, it is much easier to concentrate on learning. Afterward, we say our morning prayers together. Each child proceeds to work on a lesson independently, as I alternately work to occupy the preschoolers and help the other children with problems and questions. If it is a good day, we can be finished with our academics shortly after lunch. The children also do a number of other learning activities, such as cooking, gardening, child care, laundry, and volunteer work.

I started teaching the children how to cook at an early age so that by the age of ten they could prepare an easy meal for the family and feel proud. I also do a little catering on the side, and the children are a great help. When making meals, I usually double what is needed so the extra can be frozen for future use. We grow a large garden and can and freeze our produce. This helps our budget, and the food tastes better. For a few years we even raised and butchered our own beef.

We have been homeschooling for seven years now. Our nine children range in age from two to eighteen. The first three years I used Seton because of their excellent reputation and detailed lesson plans. As I became more experienced, I developed my own curriculum based on the Seton philosophy and work-text approach. There are so many exceptional learning products available, it is sometimes difficult to choose.

We use the *Faith and Life* series, *The New St. Joseph Baltimore Catechism*, videos of the saints, and books by Father Lovasik in the elementary grades to help form a strong base for our Catholicism. We have our own Catholic readers, which I have purchased at homeschool conferences. We use Modern Curriculum Press for phonics and math through the third grade. After that, we use *Saxon Math*. *Voyages in English* by Loyola University Press works well for us. We also use Seton's writing and spelling books. Since it is difficult enough for me just to keep up on the basics for my four elementary-age children, history, geography, and science are covered mainly by having children read the lessons themselves, check out corresponding library books and videos, and quiz each other on geography facts to be memorized. We also have a computer the children are comfortable using. It is an excellent educational tool that I hope to use to its full advantage.

I have three high-schoolers who work best in different ways. In teaching them, we have used Catholic history books purchased through TAN Books. We have the HomeQuest High School Curriculum on the computer, which has worked well to supplement their books. It has a progress check so I can see how much time has been spent on each lesson and also gives a grade for most lessons. Our eldest son has also taken a few computer classes at a local college. All in all, I try to give them access to a number of new experiences and keep them challenged.

I also wish to equip my teenagers with the tools necessary to defend their faith. We started the year reading the book *Christian Apologetics*, which I had borrowed from our pastor. For my teenagers the presentation of the arguments for the existence of God was rather deep. The book we are using now, *Covenant with Jesus*, is much easier for them to follow. It is available from the Fatima Family Apostolate. As it is definitely Catholic, it includes the points I hope to impress upon the kids. It covers the truths of our faith while instilling a more personal commitment to Jesus Christ. We also have enjoyed Scott Hahn's tape series *Answering Common Objections*, which we purchased from St. Joseph Communications.

It can be a delicate balance for parents: we want our children to stay Catholic but not to become arrogant, thinking that they are better than other people just because they are Catholic. I am impressed with the Pope's teaching that, as Christians, we must band together with people of all faiths in living out God's commandments and treating each other and our faiths with respect and dignity.

This is a busy, yet happy, time of my life, and I would not trade it for anything. My husband is a wonderful, loving father and a supportive principal. We are striving to live by God's commandments for the welfare of our souls. My husband and I are grateful to God for all the abundant blessings he has bestowed on us.

The ideal condition would be, I admit, that men should be right by instinct; but since we are all likely to go astray, the reasonable thing to do is to learn from those who can teach.

—Sophocles

The Only Child
Julie McCaskill

We were not blessed with a large family but were given the cross of infertility to bear. This cross was, and sometimes still is, difficult to carry because it was quite unexpected. We presumed that children were something you simply got if you were open to God's will. We certainly learned better. The Lord, in his goodness, allowed us to adopt our oldest son and gave us a surprise baby daughter eight years later. Needless to say, that explains the unusual spacing between the children.

Although our daughter Juliana is not technically an only child, she is the only child left at home; her brother is twenty-one and a college student. I have discovered that homeschooling an only child comes with its own unique difficulties. I have not found all the answers yet, as this is our first year home educating, but I do have a plan.

When we began homeschooling, I found out an awful truth about my daughter's previous academic life. She had learned to play the school game without gaining any real knowledge. For instance, she said to me one day, "Mom, this is the first time I have ever had to read a book for a book report. Before I just skimmed through, read the blurb on the jacket, and put together a report." My daughter was an intelligent but unmotivated student while attending school. She did not have a strong grasp of her faith, her spelling was poor, and she did not enjoy even recreational reading. Now, she is eager to learn and is not afraid to ask questions. In fact, she is becoming quite a deep thinker.

Problems with socialization are real, but surmountable. For example, I recently learned that our homeschool support group has activities for teens. The teens attend Mass and play sports once a week. My daughter and I decided to make these weekly events part of our schedule. My future plans include encouraging Juliana to invite home some of the girls she meets at these activities. Teens need time to deepen friendships. I also hope to make arrangements for fun outings. In addition, my daughter will take a class at the local recreation department. She may or may not make new friends, but at least she will be busy.

Although this has been a difficult year, I see the benefits of our work. The extra time needed to arrange social activities for my child has been worth the effort. The social situation of a homeschooled only child may not be ideal, but the academic and spiritual results are fantastic.

A little learning leads men away from the truth; a large learning confirms the truth.

—Hilaire Belloc, *Essays of a Catholic*

It Takes a Parish: Combining
Work and Homeschooling
Annie Kitching

We all want to raise our children *in the Church*. I have the great blessing of raising my children *at the church* as well! As director of religious education at a large parish, I spend at least fifty to sixty hours a week working, but thanks primarily to my supportive pastor and to the loving support of my parish, I have experienced the joy and challenge of homeschooling my son for the past two years and hope to include my daughter next year.

Having been Catholic school teachers, my husband and I assumed that our children would attend Catholic school. To our dismay, however, we found that our son, Aidan, did not blossom in the parish school as we had hoped. Somehow the school's personality and my son's learning style did not mesh. By second grade, he was no longer the enthusiastic learner he had been. He even began to resist reading for pleasure. We realized we had to do something, and in the middle of his third-grade year enrolled him in a Montessori school. His sister, Lydia, entered in the preschool class. Montessori education was an eye-opener for both my husband and me.

We came to admire the Montessori philosophy. Most of all we appreciated the one-room school setting. All grades, first through sixth, shared one classroom. This led to natural family-like interactions among the children as they learned from one another, cared for one another, and developed supportive rather than competitive relationships. The noncompetitive philosophy was an aspect we appreciated. We loved the respect accorded to parents and the understanding that children learn in all of life's situations, not just in a classroom. Also, we were elated to experience life without homework. It was delightful to spend evenings playing games or reading aloud. We no longer had to serve as homework enforcers.

But when, after sixth grade, Aidan graduated from the Montessori school, we were in a quandary. We could not face the old-style school again, but what was the alternative? We might not have thought of homeschooling had it not been for some trailblazing homeschooling parents in our parish. I had noticed some surprising differences in their children, particularly the teenagers. These homeschooled teens were not sulky, rude, or self-conscious. They seemed to have no problem looking me in the eye and speaking to me respectfully. Their attitude was impressive.

About this time the book *Hard Times in Paradise* was being read on the *Radio Reader*. It is a book about the Colfax family, whose homeschooled children went on to Harvard and Yale. At the same time, the children and I were reading aloud Louisa May Alcott's *Jack and Jill* and found, to our surprise, that the wise and gentle mother in the book decides to remove her children from school and educate them at home. In a way that could not be purely coincidental, the homeschool idea seemed to be coming at me from all directions.

Reading on the subject of home education was essential in helping us to make the final decision, and it helped me think through what we would be doing and why. I soon saw that homeschooling families vary as much as other families do and that there are all sorts of reasons to homeschool.

Understanding your own reasons is the first step to making the right decisions for your own situation. Although I respect much of the philosophy and point of view behind Mary Kay Clark's *Catholic Home Schooling*, I felt uneasy about the very structured academic approach. John Holt's unschooling philosophy intrigued me, but I realized that I am far too conservative to feel completely at ease with it.

The books that most impressed me were John Taylor Gatto's *Dumbing Us Down* and David Gutterson's *Family Matters*. These books helped me form my homeschooling philosophy. Several books by Raymond and Dorothy Moore, especially *Home Style Teaching* and *Home Grown Kids*, really clicked. They seemed to be written just for me, a conservative person with untraditional views of education. The Moores offered lots of valuable ideas and referred frequently to families who homeschool while running their own farms or businesses. I had often felt that my work at the church was not unlike a family business, being more of a lifestyle than a job. The Moore's prescription for homeschooling mixes equal amounts of academic work, volunteer service, and productive labor. The prescription resonated with me, and it was a recipe that seemed ready-made for our unique situation.

One of the things that makes homeschooling possible for our family is my working environment. Our parish's religious education offices are in a former convent, a spacious two-story brick building complete with living room, kitchen, and back yard. The goal of our staff was that the building become a family center for the parish. Having our own children present helped other parishioners feel comfortable about bringing their children by. Since my children became accustomed to being *at the convent* after school (often long into the evening, on weekends, and through the summer), extending this situation to home-schooling was not hard to imagine. My understanding pastor showed the utmost faith in me and gave me permission to give it a try. Our decision was made.

I took advantage of the Emmanuel Center, a support center for homeschoolers in the area, in putting together an eclectic curriculum. I did not feel the need to have distinctly Catholic texts, believing that I could weave faith themes throughout the lessons myself. I certainly got enough practice doing this in the Catholic school classroom.

We have had some real curriculum successes and a few flops, too. We are delighted with the *Saxon Math* series, which made a difficult subject easy to teach and learn. After some false starts in language arts, I stumbled upon the Loyola University Press *Voyages in English* program, which is perfect for my son, who needs the emphasis on composition. A less successful choice was A Beka science. I chose it for the Christian approach, but found I had to be on guard against gratuitous anti-Catholic slams. The second year I switched to what I thought was a completely inoffensive secular text. We have tried several American history texts and found there is no way to escape the relentless political correctness. We discuss the correctness as needed.

For religion we have thoroughly enjoyed Ignatius Press' *Faith and Life* series, which is solid in content and perfect for use outside a classroom. Surrounded as we are by religious material of all kinds, we have branched out a bit this year and are using *De Sales Adult Education* video series. I enjoy viewing these and discussing them with Aidan. We learn together.

The more I have loosened up, the happier I have been with the results. One form of loosening up was realizing I did not have to teach everything. Getting tutors in math and science has been a wonderful way to upgrade the instruction. These are not my best subjects. Aidan has had the opportunity of getting to know and work with some fine Catholic adults. One big advantage of my situation is knowing many people in the parish. Another form of loosening up was realizing that not all curriculum materials need to be textbooks, a former teacher's hang-up.

We particularly enjoyed using *The Book of Virtues* as seed for writing assignments, especially concentrating on "George Washington's Rules of Civility". Realizing that Aidan's spelling was weak, I brought out my college text, *Phonics for Teachers*. I still remember how much I learned from this neat little book, and Aidan has enjoyed its programmed learning format. Useful curriculum materials can be found in unexpected places. Literature is central to our lives together, and I refuse to ruin it with too much discussion and analysis as many books were ruined for me in junior high and high school. We also have the freedom to let the spirit move us. This year we have read, or listened on tape to *The Adventures of Tom Sawyer*, *The Adventures of Huckleberry Finn*, *A Connecticut Yankee in King Arthur's Court*, *Life on the Mississippi*, and *The Prince and the Pauper*. What other school would let you have as much Mark Twain as you wanted?

A big advantage of my workplace is Aidan's access to computers and the Internet. We discovered that his composition improved by leaps and bounds when he started using the computer instead of writing by hand. We also made the acquaintance of Regina Coeli Academy (RCA). This is an online distance-learning Catholic high school and can be contacted through the Internet at www.ewtn. com/rca/. Although Aidan has not yet taken a class with RCA (he will give it a try this summer), he has been welcomed as a visitor in a number of classes. The students have taken him under their collective wing, even praying for him. He frequently exclaims about how nice these RCA students are. Being on their mailing list has been an asset, too. We have greatly appreciated their "Saint of the Day". What nice e-mail to discover every morning.

I try to keep in mind that academics are not everything. The other components, service and productive labor, have been important and much easier to organize from our work environment than they would have been from home. Aidan has many opportunities to be of service around the parish. He has been a real asset around the office. He has served special Masses, braided palms for the Palm Sunday decorations, helped polish the terrazzo floors, and chopped up a fallen tree, among other things. Especially exciting has been the opportunity he has had learning about television production from watching and assisting as our parish's *Catholic Catechism* and *Catholic Customs and Traditions* series were being filmed.

As a result of this exposure, Aidan was able to obtain a paid position as one of the cameramen on the Outreach Mass Crew. Because of his flexible schedule he has also had the opportunity to work in a candy store in downtown East Lansing that is run by one of our catechists. These various work and volunteer experiences are teaching him valuable and practical lessons that are probably more useful than many academics. Of course, being a working homeschooling mom has its disadvantages. I have found that there are a few times of year when I am simply too busy to give Aidan the attention he needs. Sometimes my energy needs to go into the job.

Loosening up has helped here too. I realized that we do not have to start school the first of September. We can wait until October, when the CCD classes have gotten under way. Holy Week and the week before solemn First Communion are vacation weeks for Aidan. Our school year can be flexible; nothing stops us from taking full advantage of June, July, and August.

I have felt bad about the fact that Aidan had to learn that there are times when I will drop him like a hot potato. When the pastor calls or a troubled parent or catechist drops by, my attention must immediately shift to professional concerns, even if we are deep into a lesson. Fortunately, Aidan is old enough to comprehend this and to find some other work to do until I am free. The Montessori background has helped here. As in the Montessori school, I give Aidan a checklist each day or week, listing his assignments for all subjects. He has the freedom to make decisions about what he will do when.

The big advantage of homeschooling at work, particularly in our parish, is that Aidan has many opportunities to know and work with good Catholic role models. The pastor jokes with him, the parochial vicar lends him video games, and the adult education director depends on him for help on the computer. Aidan asked one of the assistants in my office to be his confirmation sponsor.

It has been bandied about in unfortunate ways lately, but there is truth in the motto "It takes a village to raise a child." We are glad to respond, "It is taking a parish to raise our children!"

We make a living by what we get, but we make a life by what we give.

—Winston Churchill

What We Do
Cindy Garrison

Our first year at home, we used Seton Home Study program. I liked having lesson plans and books together. It gave me the confidence and knowledge I needed for our second year of homeschooling, when I put together my own curriculum. I did my own to fit better the needs of my children. There are some subjects in which they advance rapidly and others in which they stay right on course.

The best thing that has happened through our homeschooling has been sharing in our children's educational experience. We would have missed so much if they were away at school every day. I also enjoy watching my children grow in our Catholic faith. We attend daily Mass as often as possible, and the kids are altar servers. Our parish priest is supportive, and he has been a blessing in many ways.

I have heard it said by several people that even if the best Catholic school in the state were built right next door, they would still homeschool because it is not just an education, it is a way of life. That is how we feel. We believe we are called to educate our children both academically and spiritually, and we cannot imagine doing it differently.

During the past four years we have made adjustments to curricula. Some things work; some do not. We enjoy the flexibility of homeschooling. We have taken our children on some nice educational vacations. We enjoy a wide range of community service projects, field trips, and sporting activities in addition to our book work.

Books We Use

Kindergarten through Fifth Grade
We have found the following, all available from Seton, to be helpful:

— *MCP Math*
— *Handwriting for Young Catholics*
— *Spelling for Young Catholics* through fourth grade, then *The Natural Speller*
— *Wordly Wise*
— *Map Skills*

Seton offers many workbooks as special aids. I have used *Sentence Structuring*, *Outlining Skills*, and *Organization Skills*. For reading I choose a variety. I have rented Catholic readers from Seton and used *Catholic Stories for Boys and Girls*, volumes I to IV, from Neumann Press; Mary Fabyan Windeatt saint books from TAN Books; and various classics, such as *Treasure Island, Heidi, The Adventures of Tom Sawyer, Little Women, Little House on the Prairie, Chronicles of Narnia, The Hobbit*, and books by E. B. White.

For history and science I purchase or borrow from the library books such as *Science Wizardry for Kids*, the *Eyewitness* series, and Usborne books. We also do hands-on experiments.

For religion I use the *Baltimore Catechism* (St. Joseph edition), Daughters of St. Paul religion series, The Catholic Bible, *Little Rock Scripture Study*, and attendance at weekday Mass.

Sixth Grade
Key to Math by Steven Rasmussen and Spreck Rosekrans, available from The Learning Home, is a series of six math

booklets with extra worksheets for practice in adding, subtracting, multiplication, and division.

Learning Language Arts through Literature, by Diane Welch and Susan Simpson, can be ordered from the Emmanuel Books catalog.

Our Roman Roots is available from Roman Catholic Books. It is a student's guide to Latin grammar and Western civilization.

Other Resources

We use our computer for educational games and for typing reports.

The children attend Book Buddies, a local homeschool club where they have an opportunity to give oral presentations and book reports.

My children enjoy sing-along tapes with Catholic songs, states and capitals, etc. We also listen to classical music from several composers.

All wisdom comes from the Lord and is with him for ever.

—Sirach 1:1

Preschool Montessori-Style
Kim Fry

The preschool years are especially gratifying to me, both as a mother and as a homeschooler. It is a great privilege to share in the joy that small children exude as they begin to learn about the world around them. Their enthusiasm is contagious. I am also a big fan of Maria Montessori, and her methods have served us well in the early school years. Her concept of work and play seems particularly ideal for learning at home.

The core of our homeschool, both for preschool and later years, is lots of reading. Every week we get an assortment of children's literature from the library. I get a book or two from several of the nonfiction sections, plus a few storybooks. Because young children enjoy stories with repetitive lines, such as *The Little Red Hen* and *The Gingerbread Boy*, we usually have one of that sort in our stack. It is important that you, as the reader, like the books, or you will be reluctant to read them over and over. And you will be asked!

We have found some outstanding illustrators, such as Susan Jeffers, Jan Brett, and C. W. Anderson, and we often select their books. When you have children count the birds on the pages or find the characters from the text, they stay involved with the story line. It is a simple thing to encourage dramatic play afterward. Eye-liner whiskers, a towel pinned as a cape, or a sheet tossed over a table can start great imaginative play.

We do not have a formal religion curriculum at this age.

As Catholics, we have a rich heritage to share, and one of the best ways to pass it on is to pray with the children. By saying the Angelus, setting a time for praying the Rosary (buying rosary beads for each child), and taking a moment to show the proper way to cross oneself, one can almost effortlessly teach them certain truths, while helping them form good habits.

People of all ages, especially preschoolers, thrive on consistency and rhythm. The Church recognizes this and has given us the liturgical year and the Mass. Children love a party and are eager feast-day helpers. I buy inexpensive coloring books of the saints for them to work on as I read about the saint of the day. Having a priest give them a tour of the church can make it their place too. For spiritual reading, *St. Joseph*'s little books are good and readily available. The content is sound, and the images are implanted deeply in the memory.

Montessori was a vocal advocate of life skills that lead to independence and self-confidence. These are easily mastered with everyday items at home. All my kids have been thrilled to discover that if you lay a coat or shirt upside down in front of you and place your hands in the sleeves you can slip it on right over your head. I use an old shoe of my husband's and lace it with two different colored strings to teach tying. Putting on an older sibling's shirt or belt helps children learn to button and snap. The openings are larger than on their own clothes, and the extra room makes it easy to see what they are handling.

Other tasks they can master are watering plants, dusting, and bed-making. My little people have comforters on their beds, and this helps them learn to make their beds. Drawers are labeled with pictures of their contents to remind them what goes where. Even mundane chores like laundry can be learning times. We start by having children name the item being folded, then progress to sorting into piles of white and colored clothes and pairing socks by color, pattern, and owner. They like to have me drop wet clothes into a basket so they can load the dryer. I think it is crucial to show them that you think their help is important. It is extremely important to them.

The kitchen is a treasure trove of early learning activities. There is not a child alive who does not like water play. Children transfer water from one side of a divided sink to another with a turkey baster or sponges. They fill cups from pitchers. I sometimes put a small amount of soapy water in the sink and let them wash toys. This activity has the added advantage of making little hands clean. A garbage bag with holes cut for head and arms keeps them dry.

Needless to say, food in general and cooking in particular are a big hit. Children can learn to pour rice and flour and stir with a little assistance. Playing with food coloring under supervision opens up myriad learning activities, from mixing colors to painting toast. Dried beans can be sorted into muffin tins or empty egg cartons, starting with two varieties and gradually adding more. This is best done with Mom nearby to ensure that the beans land in the tins and not in an ear. Unshelled nuts also work, and using tongs or spoons to handle them increases the challenge. Sorting by texture only, with closed eyes, should keep even the advanced child busy. Large noodles can be laced, and Cheerios strung on licorice strings make tasty necklaces.

Table-setting is ideal for teaching one-to-one correspondence, an important premath concept. Your helpers must think about how many places there will be, place one fork to each place, and so on. You can make simple place mats with pinking shears and trace the outlines of the plates and flatware for your youngest helpers. I often give my daughter the silverware rack from the dishwasher and have her sort the forks and spoons. The sharp knives are kept separately. When it's time to wash empty jars and lids, a two-year-old can be kept amused matching them up, putting the lids on, and taking them off. With a bit of thought a creative mom can find lots of possibilities in the kitchen.

Nature study plays a big part in our family. We read all the life-cycle books we can find, and these have been the mainstay of our science curriculum for the early years. We have watched how everything from butterflies to mushrooms grow. We have grown sprouts to eat and made birdfeeders out of peanut butter and seed. I should do more gardening, but I cannot quite shake the memory of an overzealous junior horticulturist uprooting a bed of newly planted annuals. He was weeding for me! Taking a magnifying glass along on walks is fun, particularly if you are not in a hurry. It is important not to forget an occasional walk after dark when possible. Nighttime provides a whole different view of the neighborhood.

The most school-like activities we do are sticker games. A wide variety of stickers are available at teacher supply stores. Armed with stickers, unlined index cards, and contact paper there is virtually no end to the games you can make. I cut a small index card in half, attach the stickers, and cover with clear contact paper. One success has been matching pairs of unlike things, such as cars and birds, and then matching pairs of like things, such as robins and bluebirds. Holy cards can be used for matching activities and for memory games. I have used the mini-stickers to make number puzzles by placing a number of stickers on the right side of a large index card and the corresponding numeral on the left. Then the card is cut down the center in wavy or zigzag lines.

We have found back issues of magazines like *Your Big Backyard* while scouting around thrift shops. We clip from these, mount the pictures on construction paper, and label them. Children can sort the animals into groups: birds, cats, habitat, things that fly, things that live in water. Old calendar art can be turned into puzzles by applying clear contact paper and cutting in random shapes. Family members can help obtain religious calendars, which are particularly nice. Old greeting cards can be covered, hole-punched, and laced with shoelaces. I have never gotten the sandpaper letters that so many books recommend, but the new puffy paints make nice raised letters to enhance the nature pictures. One can get two colors of paint and do the vowels in a contrasting color.

For whatever reason, my children are not fond of finger-painting, although mustard in a Ziplock bag has gone over well. (Put mustard in a Ziplock bag, close tightly, then let the children make designs by "drawing" on the bag with their fingers.) They have all drawn from an early age, and a favorite project is to secure a thin sheet of tracing paper over a coloring book page to trace. Collages are a big pastime at our house. We have enjoyed gluing beans to paper to make rosary pictures. We have also used ABC noodles to make the alphabet or to glue under hand-printed words. With chalk and paper you can send a pre-schooler to make rubbings of tree bark, cement, bricks, or leaves. Fabric can be cut into squares for children to mix, then sort by pattern and texture for a quiet, inside game.

Finally, one should not overlook the hardware store when shopping for preschoolers. Nuts and bolts come in all sizes and putting them together develops fine motor skills.

Washers also work well. My favorite resource is the paint sample section. These can be sorted by color or by shades of color or arranged from lightest to darkest.

We are in this together as a family, and the best way that we have found to teach is to discuss, explain, and bring the children into our daily activities as we go about them. Older children can read to preschoolers and sharpen their own skills in the process. My preschoolers sit on my lap and hold flashcards for older siblings. They draw pictures and dictate simple messages for grandparents. They play with pattern blocks and Cuisenaire rods when their big brothers and sisters are finished with them. This way of learning is a family affair. It does not require complicated lessons or an exorbitant amount of money. All it takes is a willingness to spend a few extra minutes throughout the day to take advantage of the learning opportunities already built into family life. Drawing on the graces received through the sacraments of marriage and the Eucharist makes teaching in these years eminently doable.

There are countless books on the market about pre-school education. Unfortunately, many are filled with highly artificial activities, or they push children into complicated work prematurely. I have found the ones listed below to be good, and they do not require expensive equipment.

— *Workjobs for Parents*, available from Cuisenaire (Appendix D)
— *Montessori in the Home*, by Elizabeth Hainstock
— *Do Touch*, by LaBritta Gilbert, has directions for mom-made learning materials and no busy work.
— *Montessori for Moms*, an online book you can download (www.primenet.com/~gojess/mfm/abouthtm.htm),

has directions, resources, and the famous equipment. Most creative moms can study these and improvise without downloading.

— Seton Home Study School and Catholic Heritage Curricula (see Appendix B) carry helpful preschool books.

But Jesus said, "Let the children come to me, and do not hinder them; for to such belongs the kingdom of heaven."

—Matthew 19:14

Games: Purposeful Fun
Becky Wissner

Our homeschooling has benefitted from knowledge gained from members of our homeschool group and from the involvement of the children's grandparents. We have also been helped by the people busy reprinting our Catholic treasures. I cannot imagine trying to pull together a Catholic program of study without the many resources we now enjoy. We particularly like the *Cardinal Readers*, published by Neumann Press, and *Little Stories for Little Folks*, which can be ordered from Catholic Heritage Curricula. *Old World and America*, reprinted by TAN Books, and the texts published by Seton Home Study are also useful.

I began homeschooling with this help, using a traditional work-text approach. I like the method but also enjoy adding variety to our curriculum. A balance of focused, structured study, alternated with purposeful educational games, has provided the right touch for our family. Moreover, we have discovered that we do not have to spend much money to spice our studies.

The first idea that opened my mind to the possibilities of creative learning I found in Seton's spelling books. The text recommends having students use a finger to trace words on their desks. At the same time, the children say the letters out loud, thus involving as many senses as possible. I have since used this technique to help the children perform extra repetitions in subjects like phonics and history. I have the children copy a phonogram that gives them trouble or maybe a history date. Doing so fixes the information firmly in their minds.

As I was teaching parts of speech to my children, I tired of our usual ways. It occurred to me that turning learning into a game would relieve our tedium. At first I wrote words on paper and put them in a jar. The kids drew a word and then had to tell which part of speech it was. I helped them use the words correctly in goofy sentences. Over time, and with the help of my father, it became a fun and simple game.

I drew a giant rectangle on a sheet of paper, then divided the rectangle into rows and columns to create a grid. I filled the top row with labels of the parts of speech.

Here is a small sample board:

Make a Sentence	
Noun	Verb
Draw three more cards	Use to describe hair

As you can see, I wrote activities in some of the boxes and left many blank. You can customize your own game by filling in as many of the boxes as you like, including more parts of speech, and varying the activities. I used the words, written on slips of paper, that I had made previously.

To begin a game, have the first child draw one slip of paper. The child reads the word written on the slip and decides what part of speech it is. He places the slip on the game board, covering a box, then does the activity if there is one listed. Play then passes to the next child. Play continues until the page is covered or until the children are ready for something different. With this game, children learn the parts of speech and also have fun.

I soon realized that much of our learning could be accomplished through the purposeful fun of homemade educational games. The possibilities are limitless. For example, after seeing my games, a friend, Rachel Mackson, was inspired to create homemade worksheets so her children could learn Greek letters and words. She used the Greek alphabet font on her computer to write secret messages using Greek letters.

Games are always evolving in our home. Our latest favorite is an expanded version of bingo. I make up bingo sheets filled with numbers. I call out math problems, and the children cover a number if it is the correct answer. Sometimes I let them use mini-marshmallows or chocolate chips, which they are allowed to eat when the game is over.

My father and I are planning to make a game based on the Candy Land board. We will draw a meandering path of colored squares. The children will use a game piece and roll a die to move forward. They will draw a card matching the color of the square on which they land and must answer the question listed. This should work well for math facts, and the game can be customized by changing the questions on the cards. I can also make alternate sets of cards for my children who are far apart in age.

I want to use a larger piece of posterboard for the playing surface, but a sheet of paper would work well. I like to make question cards by cutting up colored index cards. The children like to be involved and enjoy coloring the board. It is up to each individual family to decide how simple or elaborate to make a game, but I have learned that I am more likely to make things that are not too complex.

Playing games is certainly not enough for our home-school. Nonetheless, I find that balancing work-text study with educational games sustains interest and helps cover the time when my attention must be elsewhere. Initially, I must play a game with the children, but once they learn it, they can continue without me. I feel good that they are spending time on productive learning and having fun at the same time. In this way, my busy times are utilized to advantage.

Let early education be a sort of amusement; you will then be better able to find out the natural bent.

—Plato

Getting Grandparents Involved
William E. Brown

Necessity is the mother of invention. Our daughter home-schools her children, and Grandma and I get to participate. There are only eighty-five miles between our houses, so it is easy to have regular contact. We serve as teacher's aides, providing whatever study helps we can. The ideas originate with my daughter and are based on needs that develop as her children progress. We discuss these needs with her and try to turn them into useful actions.

Our first teaching aids were books. Grandma kept an eagle eye out for children's books to supplement standard texts. By prowling book sales, she continues to find a gold mine of children's textbooks and stories that teach. Then we found that I could help by making custom worksheets with the convenience of my computer. For example, I made my own math problems for the children. (Prince had ten pennies. He spent three pennies for a rose for Beauty. How many pennies did he have left?) Story characters that captivated the children helped them learn faster than mere abstractions did. Later on, clock faces became important to illustrate how space can represent time. These were easily replicated on my computer and began a second phase as the children advanced.

Time lines were next. We made lines representing the Wissner family from our daughter's marriage in 1984 to the present, showing the dates of birth of each of her four children. Other time lines covered the history of the United States from its founding. A line with centuries marked from 400 B.C. was used to enter events as the children studied them, allowing them to create their own history chronology. Another shows the Wissner and Brown family trees from grandparents to the youngest generation. The last one shows the months of the year, with one month blown up to show dates in that month.

There came a need for flashcards of the states. With the help of the *Children's Almanac of the States* and the latest *World Almanac and Book of Facts*, three-by-five flashcards were composed for each state, with vital facts on one side and an outline map of the state, with its capital marked, on the other side. The cards are used to teach recognition by shape, and games can be contrived from the information side. We have discussed an advanced game in which children would travel from state to state by correctly answering questions about an adjacent state.

Becky recently came up with a clever way to teach parts of speech. Players draw words on slips of paper from a well and place them on a game board under the proper part of speech, such as noun, pronoun, adjective, verb, adverb. Special premiums are awarded on some of the board places. In the future, play pieces might also be used to teach the diagramming of sentences.

It was a tedious job to make all those slips. Besides that, they were fragile and easily blown off the board with a child's laugh. We came up with a solution. Words, including many in conjugated forms, were typed on file folder stock, which is a good deal heavier than paper. Pages were laminated with transparent film and then sliced on a paper cutter to yield 3,100 words on half-inch by two-inch game pieces.

Our next projects will be board games involving arithmetic problems and vocabulary words and, later on, another flashcard series for countries of the world. We continue to build a little science corner of experiments and materials, which will become useful when the children are ready.

To sum up: Grandma sleuths for books and study materials. Both of us scour the Conservative Book Club monthly offerings in the homeschooling section, where we often find excellent material. I help out wherever I can be of use. We find all this fun. The reward is the priceless pleasure of seeing our grandchildren learn and grow. Such efforts also help us feel useful in our sunset years.

Being a retired grandparent is the best job in the world. That's a fact!

I can do all things in him who strengthens me.

—Philippians 4:13

Catholic Unschooling
Lynne Cimorelli

The term "unschooling" has come to represent child-led education. For me, however, unschooling is more a way of life than a methodology of education. What we do in our home is a continuation of everything we have done since our children were born, as opposed to shifting to a formal style of education at five years of age. Despite the lack of formality, we do have definite goals for our children, including:

— a good, solid understanding of their Catholic faith, which we hope will lead each of them to a lifelong, close relationship with our Savior;
— a discovery of their own unique callings while on this earth;
— possession of a good work ethic and the skills to be self-sufficient;
— a lifelong love of learning;
— the drive to find and cultivate their individual talents;
— a desire to serve others;
— the ability to vote with a conscience;
— a solid grasp of academic knowledge, including history, economics, political science, math, science, classical literature, geography, and the arts.

When the children were born, we gave them lots of love, hugs, and kisses and showed them their special place in the family. As they grew, we helped them learn to walk and talk, to dress themselves, and to discover that, as special as they are, they are not the center of the universe. As they started to ask questions, we told them about the Creator who is the center of the universe and all the wonderful things he made and our special place as humans on this beautiful planet of his. I believe that God gave us curious minds, so my method of educating is child-led. The key is to answer questions in a provocative way, in order to encourage more questions.

As soon as the children start asking, I start teaching the fundamentals of music, reading, math, religion, history, science, geography, health, political science, and more. We have always given reading a special time in our day, as we have listening to good music. As a musician, I believe in the importance of dancing with my babies and singing to them virtually all day long. This in turn leads to a curiosity about the piano, just as our reading aloud to them leads to a desire to read. We have found that noncoercive learning leads to a lifetime of pleasurable learning and a high retention of the things learned.

In music, we start with dancing and singing to the children as infants. I make up silly songs with their names and sing them many times. My twenty-one-month-old sings the end of each line. If I stop singing, she will finish the song. Before long, a child can reach the piano and start to experiment with different sounds. I let my children have free rein with the piano as long as they follow a few rules: fingers only on the keys, no pounding, and no touching the strings. We play a great deal of background music, especially classical music, which seems to calm them when they get wound up.

Around the age of three, they usually want to know how to play something, and I show them how to pick out a tune by ear. Then we move on to rhythm games and start working through music books that I wrote. However, I never force the pace. They beg me to teach them, and when I have a few minutes I will say, "Hey, I've got a few minutes right now. Would you like a piano lesson?" They always jump at the chance, which comes every few days on the average.

In my experience, reading is another skill that develops naturally. Besides reading aloud all manner of stories and nursery rhymes from the time they are born, I pull out a wooden alphabet puzzle when they are about two. My children have all been fascinated by it and have learned most of their letters just from doing the puzzle. I will hand them a letter and say, "Can you find where this *G* goes?" and while they are fitting it in, I might say, "*G* goes *guh*." In any case, the course of play flows in an unorchestrated manner. After they have learned the phonetic sounds of a few letters, I will put a couple of letters together and show them how to make a simple word like "it" or "at". Then we add more letters, and it goes from there.

I also keep a large supply of paper and crayons handy, and as their drawing gets more skilled, they always want to attempt letters. Soon they are off and writing, asking me to spell every word they can think of while I am making dinner or doing chores. I keep them each supplied with an attractive notebook, as well as their own pencils, and I often find them writing short stories and illustrating them. We have a huge library of all kinds of books in our home, from board books for the babies, to easy readers, to storybooks to read aloud, to beautiful reference books for children. All these books are kept within their reach, and they are constantly reading something.

A number of our reference books stimulate questions about the world around us. We have books on rocks, minerals, animals, plants, how things work, different historical periods, biographies, and art, to name a few. We also have a globe sitting on the kitchen counter, which is referred to quite often and prompts questions like, "Mommy, where's that country?" I find that, by answering their questions, I am giving the children more than a full curriculum of knowledge on many different grade levels.

For instance, my six- and eight-year-olds can tell you all about how plants grow from seeds, the food chain, stars, comets, asteroids, meteors, rockets, rain, clouds, the seasons, the rotation and revolution of the earth, different types of rocks and how they are formed, types of insects and what they do, mammals, reptiles, politicians, the President, Congress, how laws are made, why taxes are collected and where they go, whom not to vote for in the next election, where the U.S., South America, Africa, Hawaii, and many other places are on the globe, slavery, the American Revolution, and on and on. All this learning takes place through reading aloud books that strike their fancy and by my being available to answer questions.

One might fear that math would not be covered thoroughly enough using this approach. So far that has not been the case. With math, we start with basic counting, which the children pick up through counting fingers, toes, shoes, Lego bricks, blocks, M&M's, and anything else they come across. Then we move on to adding and subtracting these objects. At around age five, they are able to understand the concept of multiplication through grouping these objects. For example, they figure out that three pairs of shoes equal six shoes, and that this is equivalent to the equation $3 \times 2 = 6$.

I do not worry about the written representation of equations until a couple of years later, although the younger ones do tend to see what the older ones are doing, so they pick it up earlier. Even then, I do not write out many math problems. I write things out only if we are doing a word problem that gets too complex to see in the mind's eye and is more easily understood on paper. My children love mental math and ask for problems to solve at meals and in the car. They like what we call "McDonald's math". I pose the following type of question, "If we buy four Chicken McNugget Happy Meals with four nuggets each, how many chicken nuggets is that?" They love figuring the answer. We also learn fractions at lunch time while dividing oranges. With so many children, we usually split three oranges and introduce fractions at an early age. In order to get their fair share, the children need to know how many fourths are in three oranges, and sometimes how many eighths. Of course, cooking and reading recipes are great ways to learn the written representation of fractions and various equivalencies. The children must use the quarter-cup measure twice when the half-cup measure is lost or dirty!

My husband is a general contractor and often sits down with our eight-year-old son to show him how to read plans and the various ways math is used to estimate the cost of a project. He has shown him how to count doors, sinks, toilets, and the like and multiply the number by the cost; how to use one-quarter-inch and one-eighth-inch architectural scales to find the dimensions of a building and its rooms; and how to find the area of irregular rooms by expanding them into a square or rectangle, finding the area and subtracting the area of the cutouts.

The children understand the concept of earning interest on money from having a bank account and the principle of paying interest on loans from listening to their parents' conversations about taking out loans and the costs involved. I also discovered a calculus program for kids and have had fun posing various problems to them as an additional challenge.

Science is also covered well by unschooling. It is a large subject made up of a number of disciplines, such as geology, botany, astronomy, anatomy and physiology, physics, chemistry, and zoology. We have made it a point to amass a large reference library with books on most of the branches of science. These books have inspired many questions. The children are farther ahead than I had thought possible.

They have collected a huge number of rocks and identified them and learned about how they were formed (geology). They have planted gardens and identified all sorts of flowers, fruits, vegetables, and trees and observed their seasonal changes (botany). They have observed and discussed comets, eclipses, and the way moons orbit planets and planets orbit the sun (astronomy). They have studied skeletal structure, the layers of the skin, various internal organs, and the immune system (anatomy and physiology). They have seen how different things work, gravity, force, and friction (physics). They have marveled over atoms and molecules and have seen simple chemical reactions, such as baking soda and vinegar mixed to make carbon dioxide (chemistry). They have also learned about animals through raising pets and observing the wildlife in our backyard (zoology).

My son has started to use a microscope and has shown an interest in saving his money to buy a telescope. Because we are not tied to a curriculum or a long, formal school day, there is plenty of time daily for observing nature and formulating all sorts of questions. There are also a number of excellent computer programs to reinforce science, math, reading, history, and other subjects.

We teach religion by reading aloud from the Bible, the *Faith and Life* series, the *New St. Joseph Baltimore Catechism*, the *Catechism in Examples*, and stories about the saints. We also teach religion by going to Mass, by giving money, clothing, and food to the poor, and most recently by sponsoring two children from Third World countries through Catholic Child Sponsorship. We feel it is important to know both Scripture and Catholic doctrine and to show our faith by living it.

We feel that preparing for college is important. Most unschoolers find that, as the children get older, they start to define for themselves the direction in life that they want to take and naturally move toward a more structured approach in anticipation of college entrance exams and SATs. Unschooling also allows for time to explore apprenticeship options.

To demonstrate how unschooling works, let me share a sample day.

A typical day at home starts out with breakfast and chores and maybe some piano lessons. When the weather is nice, we go outside right away and explore the principles of physics by rollerblading on the hills. Then we might water the garden and check the new seedlings, feed and water the animals, look for aphids and either try to find some ladybugs to eat them or blast them off with a hose, pick wildflowers, watch the house across the street being built, and practice our French while swinging on the swing set. On days when the weather is not so nice, the children sometimes pull out their cookbooks and whip up a batch of cookies or muffins. Cooking is great practice in math and reading, as well as a little kitchen chemistry, and provides a yummy snack, too.

When we come in for lunch, we often do either a spelling or a math bee. If they want to ask about something else, we get the globe down and talk about a different part of the world and life there. I answer questions like, "Are they eating lunch right now, too? What time is it there? Is it spring there? Is it hot or cold? Do they snow-ski there? What kind of food do they eat? Do they live in a house like ours or a little hut? What kind of clothes do they wear? What language do they speak? Do they have poisonous snakes there? Does it rain a lot? Do they drive on the wrong side of the road?" and on and on.

After lunch, the babies go down for a nap, and we often read books aloud; then we will read selections from religion and from classic literature. Currently we are reading the *Little House on the Prairie* books; we have also read the *Winnie the Pooh* books, *The Lion, the Witch, and the Wardrobe*, *Charlotte's Web*, *Stuart Little*, and a number of biographies of people such as Amelia Earhart, Einstein, Mozart, Beethoven, Michaelangelo, Leonardo da Vinci, Marie Curie, Helen Keller, and Harriet Tubman.

We also enjoy fun science books like the *Magic School Bus* series. I often choose books according to the holidays coming up. When I am done reading, I like to listen to the children read a little bit to me. Often they read things to me during the course of the day, so I do not ask them to read any extra. But on occasion I will have them read a little bit of a *McGuffey's Reader*, or something similar, to be sure that their ability to decode longer words is progressing.

After we finish reading, they will run outside and play something related to our latest book. I have found them playing with the stroller as if it were the wagon in *Little*

House on the Prairie, trying to build a bird's nest the way a bird would, grinding the acorns in our yard and attempting to make bread out of them, writing hieroglyphics with sidewalk chalk, and making animal tracks in the dirt and then pretending to be big game hunters. Sometimes they try to sketch or paint a scene from the backyard. This list gives just a few of the rather creative ideas the children have come up with.

Several afternoons a week we have activities like gymnastics, karate, ballet and tap, swim team, and art classes. Some of these are ongoing, but many are seasonal or short-term classes. The children love these activities and have discovered some talents as well as new friends. We also meet with other homeschoolers for park days every once in a while. After our activities, we have dinner as a family every night, where Daddy and I often engage in lively discussions of politics, economics, his work, my new business, and anything else that strikes our fancy. The children learn a great deal from listening to their parents discuss various issues of the day. When dinner is over, it is generally time to clean up, hear a story, and go to bed.

Conclusion

I hope this sample day helps shed light on what is paradoxically an effective way to learn and yet completely at odds with the method of education the public school system uses. Home education is truly a blessing, and I treasure the time I am able to spend with my children exploring the world on their terms, adding to my own knowledge at the same time, and leading a full life based on a love of learning and an appreciation of the greatness of God and his creation.

Chapter 6

Support and
Encouragement

And let us not grow weary in well-doing, for in due season we
shall reap, if we do not lose heart.

—Galatians 6:9

Kids Speak Out

Mary (age 5)

I like homeschooling because it's fun. I like learning about the saints and drawing their pictures. I really like math. In homeschool you can never be late.

Aaron (age 8)

Homeschooling is my favorite thing to do. My mom helps me read religion books, write, do phonics and spelling. I like breaks and playing football on my lunch break. I can read *Great Moments in Football* by myself. I have read six chapters. I think you kids out there might want to try it too.

Drew (age 8)

I like homeschooling because it is fun. I like reading adventure and mystery stories. My favorite subject is math. I like being able to do things with my friends.

Eddie (age 9)

I like homeschooling because I can learn what I want when I want and I can choose how I want to learn. For instance, if I choose to study about ants, I can read about them, or I can go outside and observe them.

Also, I get to stay at home, and I know that the food I am eating is good for me.

Philip (age 9)

I like homeschooling because you can be with your family most of the time. You get to eat all your meals with them too. You get to do some workbooks that you like best. And, if you get your work done quickly, you have the rest of the time to play. You can draw and write about anything. You get to work on some of your favorite things.

Here are some of my favorite things: science, space stuff, most history, electricity, taking things apart, flying, and building, especially Legos. I also like digging holes, especially when they are bigger than me. And I like some math. In part of my spare time, I read. I love reading, especially about knights, castles, and mystery stories, but I read a lot of different kinds of books.

Nina (age 10)

I like learning about Jesus, and I also like English because we get to write stories about pictures. I like praying the holy Rosary.

Ashley (age 10)

I have been Catholic homeschooled for four years now. To me, this has been lots of fun and hard work. I like homeschooling for many reasons; here are a few.

I can get my school done in a few hours each day. The rest of the time I can do lots of different things. My great-grandparents live next door to us, and I help them sometimes with housework or gardening projects. I also read or explore outdoors.

I like the books we use because lots of them are Catholic,

and I think it is good to learn and know that God and our faith are an important part of us. Sometimes my work is hard, but my mom is always there to help me and explain things to me. We have some very interesting talks. Several times we changed books to keep things challenging.

I have lots of friends—both girls and boys of all ages. This is one of my favorite parts of homeschooling. I can do things with kids around my age, like rollerskating, playing games, riding bikes, and visiting. I also get to spend time with little kids, and they are lots of fun too.

We do lots of things to keep our Catholic faith alive. We pray together each day. I altar-serve and lector at weekday Masses. We serve at funeral dinners, go to devotions, visit nursing homes, and clean the church. All of these things help me know God is an important part of life. I am glad I am Catholic. I like my faith and like being part of my parish.

Homeschooling has made me feel responsible. I know I have to work hard and get my studies done. In my family, we all have chores to do, so I have to make sure I do that. I run errands for my mom and sometimes others. I help watch little children when I am needed at gatherings, meetings, or in the home. My mom says all these things will make me a better adult.

The most important thing I like about homeschooling is all the time I get to spend with my family and learning about the Catholic faith.

A smile must always be on our lips for any child to whom we offer help, for any to whom we give companionship or medicine. It would be very wrong to offer only our cures; we must offer to all our hearts.

—Mother Teresa

Finding Support in Cyberspace
Sandra Heinzman

This January I gathered with eighteen close friends for a Christmas party to celebrate our first-year anniversary as a group. Although we are scattered across the U.S., from such far-flung regions as Alaska and Puerto Rico, we managed to meet at 10:30 P.M. eastern standard time. We chatted for two hours and opened gifts sent to us by our secret prayer angels. Although some of us have met face to face, most of us have seen each other only via photos.

What was different about this party? Well, the main difference between this get-together and others you may be familiar with is that each of us was in her own home, sitting at her computer. Yet, at the same time, we were visiting together in a private chat room, via America Online (AOL).

All these ladies chatting together consider themselves loop friends, or fellow loopies, and all participate in an online e-mail loop. What is an e-mail loop? It is not complicated, but it can confuse the newcomer (called a newbie in cyberspeak). When anyone on the loop wants to send a message, she sends it to everyone in the group, instead of to one person. Members are free to e-mail individuals, but the bulk of the e-mail is sent to the whole group.

How do you start up an e-mail loop? There are various ways to get in touch. Our particular group formed in January 1996, when an individual on the homeschooling boards of AOL advertised for people interested in a Charlotte Mason e-mail loop. Charlotte Mason was a turn-of-the-century British educator who provided helpful advice to parents teaching and tutoring at home. We joined together to discuss her philosophy. Over the last year, our group has remained fairly constant. Occasionally, someone drops off due to temporary problems or a move, but she always seems to return eventually.

Our loop has gradually evolved into a support group through which we discuss everything and anything, not just Charlotte Mason. We have discussed books such as Susan Schaeffer Macaulay's *For the Children's Sakes*, but we have now gone far beyond book discussions. We support each other in good times and bad, including marital problems, overseas moves, problems with children, loss of jobs, homeschooling dilemmas, curriculum questions, and more.

When one loop friend was without a phone for two months, the rest of us wrote her by regular U.S. mail (known online as snail mail). Some even sent letters and care packages with goodies and presents. When another loop friend had marital problems, the rest of the group organized a 24-hour, round-the-clock, prayer vigil. Each person prayed for two 30-minute periods a day. What a blessing and how powerful.

By now, we can bring up any topic, and the others will be there for support or comment. To top it off, last fall we exchanged family photographs. What fun it was to see, at last, the faces that go with the names. Naturally, we exchanged Christmas letters, which led to the party.

Our e-mail loop is like having a support group meeting every day, except that we meet at our individual convenience and do not have to be properly dressed or leave our homes. Many of us respond to messages every day, some choose to respond less frequently, and others look on. I still get a thrill when, upon signing on, I hear the bell ring, see the flag on my AOL mailbox go up, and hear the words, "You've got mail!"

In addition to e-mail loops, there are Catholic homeschooling listservs. A listserv is similar to an e-mail loop, except the mail is directed by a computer. There is no need to keep track of twenty or twenty-five separate addresses. The listserv's computer can also allow you to access a library where valuable information, such as homeschooling resources, is stored. You can also receive a synopsis of the week's e-mail rather than individual messages.

If you do not wish to receive mail, there are other options for support online. AOL has numerous homeschooling boards. There are three main forums: Homeschool Connection, *Practical Homeschooling*, and the *Home Education Magazine* (HEM). Each of these forums has about fifty message folders. There are so many folders that it would be impossible to list them all, but here are some examples:

    Unschooling
    Homeschooling a Houseful
    Homeschooling an Only Child
    Structured Homeschooling
    Semi-Structured Homeschooling
    Eclectic Homeschooling
    Classical Education
    Masterful Math
    Language Arts
    Foreign Languages
    Science
    Military Homeschooling

Homeschooling Overseas
Single-Parent Homeschooling

In addition, there is a homeschool board for Catholics in the Religious Forum. There are many websites on the Internet for homeschooling that you can easily access (see Appendix C).

Now that I have my e-mail loops and online support, I no longer feel I am alone in my homeschooling. I enjoy socializing with my local friends, but I find that my loop pals provide an invaluable addition to my life. Between my computer resources and annual homeschooling conventions, I am in homeschool overload, and I love it!

Basic scientific research, as well as applied research, is a significant expression of man's dominion over creation. Science and technology are precious resources when placed at the service of man and promote his integral development for the benefit of all. By themselves however they cannot disclose the meaning of existence and of human progress. Science and technology are ordered to man, from whom they take their origin and development; hence they find in the person and in his moral values both evidence of their purpose and awareness of their limits.

—*Catechism of the Catholic Church*, no. 2293

From Grade School Teacher to Homeschool Teacher

Colleen Wheat

I often hear, "Oh, you used to be a teacher. I don't have a problem with *you* homeschooling. It is those other people who think they can teach and have no background in education who shouldn't homeschool."

Believe it or not, my teacher's certificate has not prepared me to be a better teacher to my children. It is the gift of motherhood that prepared me for this endeavor.

As a grade-school teacher, I spent much of my day preparing paperwork, performing crowd control, and managing time. A classroom of twenty-five youngsters is a classroom of twenty-five unique individuals, all with different learning styles; this scenario did not always lend itself to effective teaching. It was a challenge to reach every student, and teaching sometimes became secondary. I would try to get my students' attention, teach them, then assign some sort of activity so that I could assess how much they had absorbed. Meanwhile, I had to wait for this one to finish, keep that one focused, and stop those three from chatting. A few students got left behind, while a few others found themselves bored because they were ahead. It was a difficult task to keep every student focused, disciplined, and learning.

I have found home education to be more efficient. Any discipline problems are handled immediately. After all, there is no need to send a note home to Mom and Dad.

Time is not lost at the beginning of the school year with assessments, as I already know exactly what the children have learned. When we do formal schoolwork, I can immediately see if they do or do not understand. I have time to reteach and reinforce. If my son is not grasping a particular concept, we can work on it until he understands; likewise, if he is flying through today's lesson plan, there is no need to hold him back. When things are going splendidly, we are not forced to stop at the top of the hour to change classes or head out to recess. We can keep working and learning. And if it is "one of those days", a rare occurrence, we can take our break a little early or schedule an impromptu field trip to the science museum or library.

As a home educator, I spend the major portion of my day with two of the people I love most, my children. There is teaching going on in all that we do. When they see me engaging in adult conversations, kneeling in prayer, or caring for our pets, they are learning. Just as I taught them to walk, talk, and say "please", I will teach them reading, 'riting, 'rithmetic, and religion. As a home teacher, I have access to a wealth of curricula that meet my children's needs. I am not restricted to using only what the administration has chosen for the entire district. I am able to pick and choose time-tested curricula that work for our particular learning style. Truthfully, the most important subject I teach is living a Christian life, and that lesson is always being taught.

All in all, I would say that there was little in my education classes that prepared me to be a homeschool teacher. As a result, I feel that anyone who truly wants to can homeschool.

Confessions of a Reluctant Homeschool Dad

David C. Mackson

As a father presently homeschooling or one about to, there are some things you can count on. First, life as you know it will change. You will question your motives for homeschooling, and some of your family and friends will think you are nuts. You will come home to a messier house and sometimes to a stressed-out wife. Some of these things you get used to, some just fade away, but when the results of your success come to fruition, none of them matter.

I always thought that, academically, homeschooling should be equivalent to, if not superior to, public school. Books and materials are readily available. I was confident that, at least through junior high, homeschooling would be no problem. Then, for high school, we parents could stay several lessons ahead as needed. My wife and I are college graduates, but being motivated parents has proven more valuable to our homeschooling success. A reasonably intelligent parent can quickly find any help needed.

Nevertheless, I was reluctant to start homeschooling because of the socialization issue and an admittedly selfish image of my son as a future football star in high school. Giving up the socialization issue was a slow process. Would our kids be freaks or outcasts? Would the kids on our street think of us as weirdos and not want to do anything with our children? Would the people at church hold up crosses toward us when we approached? Well, nothing serious happened. Do not get me wrong—some people were taken aback, but the number of these people is decreasing. I will state for the record that our children are no social misfits.

It does take time and is not always easy, but we do make sure that the children have plenty of social experiences. We spend a lot of time at Irish step dancing lessons or choir practice, since these activities are independent of school attendance. We also go to the church doughnut hour and spend time with other homeschooling people. We get together with relatives as often as we can. These activities are important. They give the children time to play and work with others, a necessary life process.

I find that our children can relate to *all* ages. We should rethink the concept of socializing kids by having them spend seven hours a day with children of the same age. It is a practice brought recently into our society, and it has not been a resounding success. And, of course, same-age socialization ends shortly after one enters the work force at the age of twenty-one or twenty-two.

What you eventually find is that you enjoy taking charge of the socialization of your children and cannot imagine why you would want the public or private school system to handle that responsibility for you.

A messy house when you come home from work is a given. Your wife, besides taking care of the kids' basic needs (a full-time job on its own), is now also fully accountable for their education. You must expect that some things will not get done. If you cherish home-cooked meals, learn to use the oven. Learning the value of simplicity is also helpful. The less you have, the less to put away. Children do not need the latest and greatest toy or learning gizmo. Having an orderly home is more important and significant to a child in the long run. Teach your kids to clean! My five-year-old does the dishes. It takes her thirty minutes to do five dishes, but I can be doing something else in the meantime, and chores teach responsibility and pride in a job well done.

You as father must be supportive. Parents must be totally united in their commitment. (If the truth be known, things started going smoothly when I got behind home-schooling one hundred percent.) You are needed by both your wife and your children. Be a friend and advisor to your wife. She may need to talk to an adult after homeschooling all day.

How do you deal with relatives who may think you have gone off your rocker? Have the strength of your convictions and the courage to put up with the disapproval. I come from a family of teachers. I must say that after a short period of skepticism they learned to accept homeschooling and now see that my children are perfectly normal.

Homeschooling can become a way of life for you as it has for us. Attitude is everything. Spending time with your children and teaching them are habits. Reading to them at night, cleaning, religion, and prayer are all part of the growing and learning process, a process you will be thankful you were there to see.

The family is the first school of those social virtues which every society needs.

—Pope John Paul II, *Familiaris Consortio*

APPENDIX A

Catholic Curriculum Providers

There are some wonderful resources available for home educators. At first you may feel you are all alone, then suddenly you are overwhelmed by the amount of support out there. The following resource guide lists Catholic merchants. By using these companies, you do not have to worry about the content of their products.

Many of these businesses are run by Catholic home educators. Their motivation runs deeper than financial success. It is a labor of love.

—Maureen Wittmann

Catholic Heritage Curricula (CHC), formerly Catholic Heritage Games, offers alternatives to secular texts. Their products have a very rich Catholic feel to them, and many are exclusives. Catholic phonics, history, art, and more are offered. They also carry some great hands-on products, such as nun dolls, Marian apparition cards, and Catholic games. The service is very fast.

CATHOLIC HERITAGE CURRICULA
(800) 490-7713
P.O. Box 125
Twain Harte, CA 95383-0125
e-mail: chc@sonnet.com

Catholic Home-Schoolers' Bookshelf has homeschooling resource books available. Religious texts include the *Lives of the Saints*, prayers and devotions, encyclicals and Church documents, Bible study, and catechisms. Phonics, Catholic literature, Latin, and more are offered.

CATHOLIC HOME-SCHOOLERS' BOOKSHELF
(540) 586-4898
2399 Cool Springs Road
Thaxton, VA 24174

Emmanuel Books offers *Greenleaf Guides and Study Packs*. Emmanuel reviews these guides and does not offer those that may be offensive to Catholics. The history section is wonderful. The language arts section includes *MCP Phonics, AlphaPhonics, McGuffey's Eclectic Readers, Little Angel Readers, English from the Roots Up*, the *Dover Thrift Edition Classics*, *The Chronicles of Brother Cadfael*, and more, more, more. Foreign language tapes and books, including Latin, are available. Math selections include *Saxon Math*, Modern Curriculum Press, and Calculadder. Also available are science, music, art, and drama curricula as well as homeschooling resource books.

EMMANUEL BOOKS
(800) 871-5598
(302) 325-9515 (fax)
P.O. Box 321
New Castle, DE 19720
e-mail: emmanuelbook@erols.com

Kolbe Academy Home School offers a classical education. The books used in their home study program are available for purchase. Their *Recommended Reading List* is a must for the price!

KOLBE ACADEMY HOME SCHOOL
(707) 255-6499
(707) 255-1581 (fax)
1600 F Street
Napa, CA 94559

The Learning Home is committed to providing curricula for the special-needs child, specifically ADD/ADHD and dyslexia. They carry material from companies such as Cuisenaire, Miquon Math, Critical Thinking Press, K'nex, and Common Sense Press. Although many of the materials offered are secular, they feature Catholic homeschooling mothers as their reviewers. The full line of Tomie de Paola books are also available from The Learning Home.

THE LEARNING HOME
(410) 536-5990
(410) 242-7826 (fax)
5573 Ashbourne Road
Baltimore, MD 21227
e-mail: learninghome@aol.com

Our Father's House carries educational materials for Catholic families, including *Miniature Mass Kit for Children, The ABC's of Christian Culture, Beginning Latin, Latin Prayers of the Mass and Rosary,* and *Faith and Life* catechisms.

OUR FATHER'S HOUSE
(206) 725-9026
(206) 725-7214 (fax)
5530 South Orcas Street
Seattle, WA 98118

Saints & Scholars has a large literature section, science, math (including *Saxon Math*), Catholic history, fun books, and a wide variety of Latin programs. The best part is that there is no charge for shipping and handling if you place a large order.

SAINTS & SCHOLARS
(800) 452-3936, orders only
(828) 452-3932
34 North Main Street
Waynesville, NC 28786

From Seton Education Media many of the same books used in Seton's Home Study Program are available for individual purchase. You can count on Catholic content in most of their books. They are currently rewriting those books that do not have a Catholic ethos to them. Several texts are available exclusively from Seton. They now offer books with four-color printing.

SETON EDUCATION MEDIA
(540) 636-9996
1350 Progress Drive
Front Royal, VA 22630

Catholic Homeschool
Resource Guide

Schools

KOLBE ACADEMY HOME SCHOOL
(707) 255-6499
1600 F Street
Napa, CA 94559

MOTHER OF DIVINE GRACE SCHOOL
Independent Study Program
(608) 348-6976
P.O. Box 1440
Ojai, CA 93024

OUR LADY OF THE ROSARY SCHOOL
(502) 348-1338
116 1/2 North Third Street
Bardstown, KY 40004

SAINT MICHAEL THE ARCHANGEL ACADEMY
(714) 730-9114
4790 Irvine Boulevard, Suite 105–286
Irvine, CA 92620
SMAcademy@aol.com

SAINT THOMAS AQUINAS ACADEMY
(209) 522-3477
1509 Chapala Way
Modesto, CA 95355
e-mail: Staa.yonon@juno.com

SETON HOME STUDY SCHOOL
(540) 636-9990
1350 Progress Drive
Front Royal, VA 22630

Books

Laura M. Berquist, *Designing Your Own Classical Curriculum: A Guide to Catholic Home Education*, Third Edition (Ignatius Press)

Mary Kay Clark, *Catholic Home Schooling: A Handbook for Parents* (Seton Home Study School Press)

Francis Crotty, *Implementation of Ignatian Education in the Home* (booklet, Kolbe Academy)

Kimberly Hahn and Mary Hasson, *Catholic Education: Homeward Bound. A Useful Guide to Catholic Home Schooling* (Ignatius Press)

Edward N. Peters, *Home Schooling and the New Code of Canon Law* (booklet, Christendom College Press)

National Support Organizations

CATHOLIC HOMESCHOOL NETWORK OF AMERICA
(CHSNA)
P.O. Box 6343
River Forest, IL 60305-6343

NATIONAL ASSOCIATION OF CATHOLIC
HOME EDUCATORS (NACHE)
P.O. Box 787
Montrose, AL 36559-0787

TRADITIONS OF ROMAN CATHOLIC HOMESCHOOLING
(TORCH)
(717) 271-0244 / (717) 271-0480 (fax)
1306 Christopher Court
Bel Air, MD 21014
e-mail: strombergj@aol.com

Magazines

Catholic Home Educator
(Father John Hardon, spiritual advisor)
P.O. Box 787
Montrose, AL 36559-0787

Heart, Mind, and Soul
(517) 349-6389 (fax or leave message)
P.O. Box 198
Okemos, MI 48805-0198

Sursum Corda!
(contains a 16-page homeschool spread)
(970) 493-8781
1331 Red Cedar Circle
Fort Collins, CO 80524

Newsletters

The Domestic Church
(CHSNA)
P.O. Box 6343
River Forest, IL 60305-6343

Homefront
525 Shadowridge Drive
Wildwood, MO 63011-1707
e-mail: Gilhaus@aol.com

Traditions of Roman Catholic Homeschooling
(TORCH)
1306 Christopher Court
Bel Air, MD 21014

Catalogs: Curriculum

CATHOLIC HERITAGE CURRICULA (CHC)
(800) 490-7713
P.O. Box 125
Twain Harte, CA 95383-0125

CATHOLIC HOME-SCHOOLERS' BOOKSHELF
(540) 586-4898
2399 Cool Springs Road
Thaxton, VA 24174

EMMANUEL BOOKS
(800) 871-5598 / (302) 325-9515 (fax)
P.O. Box 321
New Castle, DE 19720

KOLBE ACADEMY
(707) 255-6499 / (707) 255-1581 (fax)
1600 F Street
Napa, CA 94559

THE LEARNING HOME
(410) 536-5990 / (410) 242-7826 (fax)
5573 Ashbourne Road
Baltimore, MD 21227
e-mail: learnghome@aol.com

OUR FATHER'S HOUSE
(206) 725-9026 / (206) 725-7214 (fax)
5530 South Orcas Street
Seattle, WA 98118

SAINTS & SCHOLARS
(800) 452-3936, orders only
(828) 452-3932
34 North Main Street
Waynesville, NC 28786

SETON EDUCATION MEDIA
(540) 636-9996
1350 Progress Drive
Front Royal, VA 22630

Curriculum Vendors

CASTLEMOYLE BOOKS
Spelling Power
(888) SPELL-TOO (orders only)
(425) 787-2714 (inquiries)
6701 180th Street SW
Lynnewood, WA 98037
e-mail: beverly@castlemoyle.com

ECCE HOMO PRESS
Catholic Girls of the USA series
(717) 271-0240
100 Church Street
Danville, PA 17821
e-mail: EcceHomoPr@aol.com

THE INSTITUTE FOR EXCELLENCE IN WRITING
Teaching Writing: Structure and Style
(800) 856-5815
1420 South Blaine, D-103
Moscow, ID 83843

MAGNUS DOMINUS
Catholic Home Education Planner
(502) 484-0901
P.O. Box 630
Owenton, KY 40359
e-mail: Magdom@mis.net

STONE TABLET PRESS
Little Angel Readers
(314) 343-4244
12 Wallach Drive
Fenton, MO 63026-4964

WOOLY LAMB PUBLISHERS
History Links Unit Study
(360) 263-6568
P.O. Box 662
La Center, WA 98629
e-mail: little@worldaccessnet.com

Catalogs: General

BETHLEHEM BOOKS
(readers and children's books)
(800) 757-6831
15605 Country Road 15
Minto, ND 58261

COUPLE-TO-COUPLE LEAGUE
(Catholic family life and home education)
(800) 745-8252
P.O. Box 111184
Cincinnati, OH 45211-9985
e-mail: CCLI@CCLI.org

FAMILY LIFE CENTER
(800) 705-6131
P.O. Box 6060
Port Charlotte, FL 33949

FAMILY RESOURCE CENTER
Video Lending Library
(309) 637-1713
321 Main Street
Peoria, IL 61602

FATIMA FAMILY APOSTOLATE
(apologetics and more)
(800) 213-5541 / (605)472-4113 (fax)
P.O. Box 55
Redfield, SD 57469
e-mail: fatimafambks@basec.net

GILHAUS COMMUNICATIONS
(314) 458-6059 (fax)
525 Shadowridge Drive
Wildwood, MO 63011-1707
e-mail: Gilhaus@aol.com

IGNATIUS PRESS
(books and videos)
(800) 651-1531
P.O. Box 1339
Fort Collins, CO 80522-1339

LEAFLET MISSAL COMPANY
(Catholic supplies)
(800) 328-9582
976 West Minnehaha Avenue
Saint Paul, MN 55104

LOYOLA UNIVERSITY PRESS
(school supplies)
(800) 621-1008
3441 North Ashland Avenue
Chicago, IL 60657

NEUMANN PRESS
(readers and children's books)
(800) 746-2521 / (320) 732-3858 (fax)
Route 2, Box 30
Long Prairie, MN 56347

OUR LADY'S ROSARY MAKERS
(rosary-making supplies)
(502) 968-1434
4611 Poplar Level Road
P.O. Box 37080
Louisville, KY 40233

PAULINE BOOKS AND MEDIA
(children's books and catechisms)
(800) 876-4463
50 Saint Paul's Avenue
Jamaica Plain, MA 02130-3491

ROMAN CATHOLIC BOOKS
(970) 490-2735
P.O. Box 2286
Fort Collins, CO 80522-2286

ST. JOSEPH COMMUNICATIONS
(Catholic audio tapes)
(813) 868-3549 / (813) 863-3600 (fax)
P.O. Box 720
West Covina, CA 91793
e-mail: tom@saintjoe.com

SOPHIA INSTITUTE PRESS
(beautiful artwork and books)
(800) 888-9344
Box 5284
Manchester, NH 03108
e-mail: SIPress@grolen.com

TAN BOOKS
(800) 437-5876
P.O. Box 424
Rockford, IL 61105
e-mail: tan@tanbooks.com

WOMEN FOR FAITH AND FAMILY
(314) 863-8385 / (314) 863-5858 (fax)
Box 8326
Saint Louis, MO 63132

Testing

California Achievement Tests
(similar to Iowa Basic Skills)
    Seton Home Study School
    (540) 636-9990
    e-mail: testing@setonhome.org

Stanford Achievement Tests
    Kolbe Academy Home School
    (707) 255-6499
    e-mail: kolbe@community.net

Magazines: Catholic Family

The Catholic Hearth (family)
Neumann Press
(800) 746-2521
Route 2, Box 30
Long Prairie, MN 56347
e-mail: neumann@rea-lap.

Go Forth in His Name (children's)
(541) 269-5059
1575 Greenacres
Coos Bay, OR 97420

Hearts Aflame (teen)
Blue Army
P.O. Box 976
Washington, NJ 07882

My Friend (children's)
Pauline Books and Media
(800) 836-9723
50 Saint Paul's Avenue
Jamaica Plain, MA 02130-3491

St. Joseph Messenger (family)
(513) 661-7009
P.O. Box 11260
Cincinnati, OH 45211-0260
e-mail: stjoseph@erinet.com

You (teen)
(818) 991-1813
29963 Mulholland Highway
Agoura Hills, CA 91301

APPENDIX C

Catholic Websites

The Internet can be an invaluable resource for home educators. My children's babysitter, Suzanne Hunter, a thirteen-year-old, homeschooled girl, once told me that she planned to homeschool her children when she became a mother, not for the same reasons as her own mother, but because it was the wave of the future. She believes that site-based education will be obsolete by the time she is an adult. It is possible that the current advancements in technology will change the way America educates her children. Only time will tell. Until then, enjoy these websites!

—Maureen Wittmann

Websites: Schools

Kolbe Academy
http://www.community.net/~kolbe

L.P.H. Resource Center
http://www.netaxs.com/~rmk/lph.html

Our Lady of the Rosary School
http://www.bardstown.com/%7Eolrs

Regina Coeli Academy
http://www.ewtn.com/rca

Saint Thomas Aquinas Academy
http://www.staacademy.qpg.com

Seton Home Study School
http://www.setonhome.org

Websites: Homeschool Resources

Castlemoyle Publishing
http://www.castlemoyle.com

Catholic Heritage Curricula
http://www.sonnet.com/chc

Catholic Homeschool Network of America (CHSNA)
http://www.geocities.com/Heartland/8579/chsna.html

Catholic Homeschool Resources
http://www.geocities.com/Athens/Academy/6823/
mercy.html

Catholic Homeschoolers of Texas
http://www.geocities.com/Athens/Delphi/5329/
Index2.html

Emmanuel Books
http://www.emmanuelbooks.com

Heart, Mind, and Soul
http://www.geocities.com/Heartland/Village/2500

The Institute for Excellence in Writing
http://www.writing-edu.com

Magnus Dominus
http://www.users.mis.net/~kaelin/MagDom/
magnus.html

National Association of Catholic Home Educators
(NACHE)
http://www.nache.org

Traditions of Roman Catholic Homeschooling
(TORCH)
http://www.Catholic-homeschool.com

Wooly Lamb Homepage/History Links Unit Study
http://www.worldaccessnet.com/~little/welcome.html

Websites: General

Apostleship of Prayer
http://www.cin.org/ap

Bethlehem Books
http://www.catholicity.com/Market/BBooks/
default.html

Blue Army
http://www.bluearmy.com

Catholic Answers
http://www.catholic.com

Catholic Digest
http://www.catholicdigest.org

Catholic Educator's Resource Center
http://www.catholiceducation.org

The Catholic Encyclopedia
http://www.knight.org/advent/cathen/cathen.htm

The Catholic Goldmine!
http://www.catholicgoldmine.com

Catholic Information on Internet, CICI Home Page—
Catholic.Net
http://www.catholic.net

Catholic Resources on the Net
http://www.cs.cmu.edu/People/spok/catholic.html

Catholic Tradition
http://www.catholictradition.org

A CatholiCity!
http://www.catholicity.com

Christendom College Press
http://www.christendom.edu/press.html

Daughters of Saint Paul, Pauline Books and Media
http://www.pauline.org

EWTN Global Network
http://www.ewtn.com

Gregorian Chant Home Page
http://www.music.princeton.edu/chant_html

The Holy See, Official Vatican Website
http://www.vatican.va

Ignatius Press
http://www.ignatius.com

The Immaculate Heart of Mary
http://www.immaculateheart.com

Leaflet Missal
http://www.leafletmissal.org

Liguori Publications
http://www.liguori.org

The Monastery of Christ in the Desert
http://www.christdesert.org/pax.html

Neumann Press
http://www.rea-alp.com/~neumann

Order of Saint Benedict
http://www.csbsju.edu/osb

Our Sunday Visitor
http://www.oursundayvisitor.com

St. Joseph Communications
http://www.saintjoe.com

St. Joseph Messenger
http://www.aquinas-multimedia.com/stjoseph

Sophia Institute Press
http://www.sophiainstitute.com

TAN Books
http://www.tanbooks.com

The Teresian Carmel
http://www.ocd.or.at/eng/ocd.htm

Vatican Exhibit Rome Reborn
http://sunsite.unc.edu/expo/vatican.exhibit/
Vatican.exhibit.html

Women for Faith and Family
http://www.catholicity.com/cathedral/womenff

Websites: Catholic Children and Teens

Life on the Rock
http://www.ewtn.com/rock/index.htm

My Friend
http://www.pauline.org/myfriend/mfwelcome.htm

National Life Teen
http://www.lifeteen.org

You Magazine
http://www.youmagazine.com

Young Saints Club
http://www.geocities.com/Athens/1619

APPENDIX D

Math Resource Guide

This list is not complete. I have included programs that I personally like as well as programs popular with other homeschoolers. I list only programs that sell answer keys or teacher manuals to parents.

—Rachel Mackson

Math Programs

Frank Schaeffer Basic Math
These arithmetic workbooks are available at many teacher stores and are inexpensive.

The Key To Math series of workbooks
This series is deservedly popular. Each set is divided into several workbooks and has clear directions and under-standable explanations. They can be purchased from The Learning Home.

Math-U-See
This is an understanding-based program that uses manipulatives. People who find *Saxon Math* too dry often love this resource. It comes with instructional videos that make it expensive. *Math-U-See* is showing up in more home-schooling catalogs.

Miquon Math
This hands-on, understanding-based program uses Cuisenaire rods. Students write little and do not drill math facts. It is available from The Learning Home.

Modern Curriculum Press Math (MCP)
These basic math workbooks are available from Seton and Emmanuel Books. We like these in the younger grades, but do not attempt to do every problem or every page. The teacher's manuals are helpful but not strictly necessary.

Problem Solving in Mathematics (Lane County Mathematics Project)
This is a wonderful resource, available from Dale Seymour. The directions and solutions are in the workbook. It has interesting math problems and ideas on how to solve them. It is listed by grades (fourth through eighth), but you can use one volume with several grades.

Scott Foresmann Exploring Math
This text presents creative modern math, although it is a workbook, (800) 554-4411.

Supplements

By no means do you need all of these and certainly not the first year you homeschool. Build slowly.

Critical Thinking, by Dale Seymour, covers the same material as the *Building Thinking Skills* series but is less expensive, and it includes an answer key. It has many of the thinking skills on standardized and IQ tests.

Hands-On Math: Manipulative Activities for the Classroom, by Creative Teaching Press, is available for kindergarten/first grade (ISBN 30554-0260-0) and for second/third grade (ISBN 30554-0260-1). They are packed with suggested activities. Better yet, black and white reproducibles are included at the end of the book: for example, a page of paper Cuisenaire rods for the teacher to copy, color, and cut out. *Hands-On Math* provides an inexpensive alternative for those who want to liven up home math studies. It is available at many teachers' stores.

Math Wizardry for Kids is filled with fun, "wow!" activities. It is readily available at bookstores.

Mathematical History—Activities, Puzzles, Stories, and Games has a math history story on the front of each page and on the back a related puzzle or problem. It provides an easy way to add enrichment for those using a standard textbook. It is published by the National Council of Teachers of Mathematics and is available in the Bright Ideas Catalog.

Mathematicians Are People Too includes short, easy-to-read biographies of famous mathematicians. It has some political correctness thrown in, but it is worthwhile. It can be used as a read-aloud with early elementary children or can be read independently by children in fourth grade and up. Available from Dale Seymour.

Number Stories of Long Ago, reprinted from 1915, tells in story form of the discovery of numbers. It starts with simple concepts and ends up with complex ideas. Younger children might not fully understand. Just save the end for later years. It is by the National Council of Teachers of Mathematics and is available in the Bright Ideas Catalog.

Books for Parents

All the Math You'll Ever Need, by Steve Slavin, gives clear, concise explanations of basic math and provides simple algebra exercises. It is designed as a refresher course, but parents who do not use a textbook can use *All the Math* as an outline. Available at any bookstore.

Historical Topics for the Mathematical Classroom includes lots of information but is somewhat dry. It is produced by the National Council of Teachers of Mathematics and is available in the Bright Ideas Catalog.

A History of Mathematics, by Carl B. Boyer, a classic one-volume history of mathematics, is readable and scholarly. It makes a good reference. I browse through this book periodically and have found the information useful.

Journey through Genius, by William Dunham, covers a selection of great mathematical problems. The chapters open with a historical explanation followed by a formal math proof. Available at any bookstore.

The Joy of Mathematics, by Theoni Pappas, is a well-written book for grades seven and up, but makes good reading for adults too. Available from Dale Seymour.

Several Good Math Catalogs

Bright Ideas
    (800) 451-7450

Dale Seymour
    (800) 872-1100

The Learning Home
    (410) 536-5990

Heart, Mind, and Soul, a magazine published by Cindy Garrison and Rachel Mackson, includes tips, ideas, and resources for educating in the heart of the home. It features regular columns with special sections on how to teach academic subjects. What an inspiration for Catholic homeschoolers! Product reviews, and more! It is published quarterly and is only $15.00 per year; $4.00 for a sample issue (price subject to change).

Heart, Mind, and Soul
P.O. Box 198
Okemos, MI 48805-0198
(517) 349-6389 (fax or leave a message)
http://www.geocities.com/Heartland/Village/2500
e-mail: rcgarrison1@juno.com